AF595802

25

Journal of Landscape Architecture

2017

KERB ACKNOWLEDGES THE ABORIGINAL AND TORRES STRAIT ISLANDER PEOPLE OF AUSTRALIA.

WE ACKNOWLEDGE THE WURUNDJERI AND THE LARGER KULIN NATION AS TRADITIONAL CUSTODIANS OF THE LANDS ON WHICH RMIT UNIVERSITY IS LOCATED.

WE PAY OUR RESPECTS TO ANCESTORS AND ELDERS PAST, PRESENT AND FUTURE.

KERB IS COMMITTED TO HONOURING AUSTRALIAN ABORIGINAL AND TORRES STRAIT ISLANDER PEOPLES' UNIQUE CULTURES AND RELATIONSHIPS TO THE LAND, WATERS AND SEAS.

••

Kerb is published annually by:
Uro Publications
Melbourne, Australia
uropublications.com.

ISBN 978-0-6484355-5-6
ISSN 1324-8049

All rights reserved. No part of this publication may be reproduced or transmitted in any form or by any means, electronic or mechanical, including photocopy, recording or any other information or storage system, without prior permission in writing from the publisher. Any copy of this journal issued by the publisher is sold subject to the condition that it shall not by way of trade or otherwise be lent, resold, hired out or otherwise circulated without the publisher's prior consent in any form or binding or cover other than that in which it is published and without a similar condition including these words being imposed on a subsequent purchaser.

Printed in Singapore.

Distributed in Australia by Books at Manic and internationally by Idea Books.

Articles, photography, images © retained by the authors or original owners.

Disclaimer
The opinions expressed in **Kerb** Issue 25 are those of the authors and are not endorsed by the editorial team, the publisher or RMIT University.

Each edition of **Kerb** is produced by a new student editorial team.

••

Editors
Amélie Touboul
Bronwyn Geddes
Frances Shuttleworth
Jia Jia
Nina Middleton
Sonja Lutz

Editorial board
Charles Anderson - **Kerb** 25 Supervisor
Michaela Prescott

Production consultants
Marianne Dela Roza - **Kerb** 25 Transcriber
Frances Madigan - **Kerb** 25 Copy Editor

••

Art direction
Sean Hogan - Trampoline Design.
trampoline.net.au

Graphic design
A collaboration between the editors and Sean Hogan - Trampoline Design.

Acknowledgments
The editors would like to thank everyone involved in the production of the journal for their generous assistance and support during the process of this publication.

••

FRONT COVER AND SECTION DIVIDERS

JESS JOHNSON

Johnson's drawing and installation practice is influenced by the speculative intersections across language, science fiction, culture and technology. In her drawings she depicts complex worlds that combine densely layered patterns, objects and figures within architectural settings. Johnson's drawings are often displayed within constructed environments that act as physical portals into her speculative worlds. Her recent video collaborations with Simon Ward have involved translating her drawings into animated virtual reality, thus enabling her audience to have the simulated experience of entering the hypnotic realms depicted in her drawings. A selection of Johnson's artwork features on the cover of Kerb 25 and throughout the journal.

Landscape
Architecture

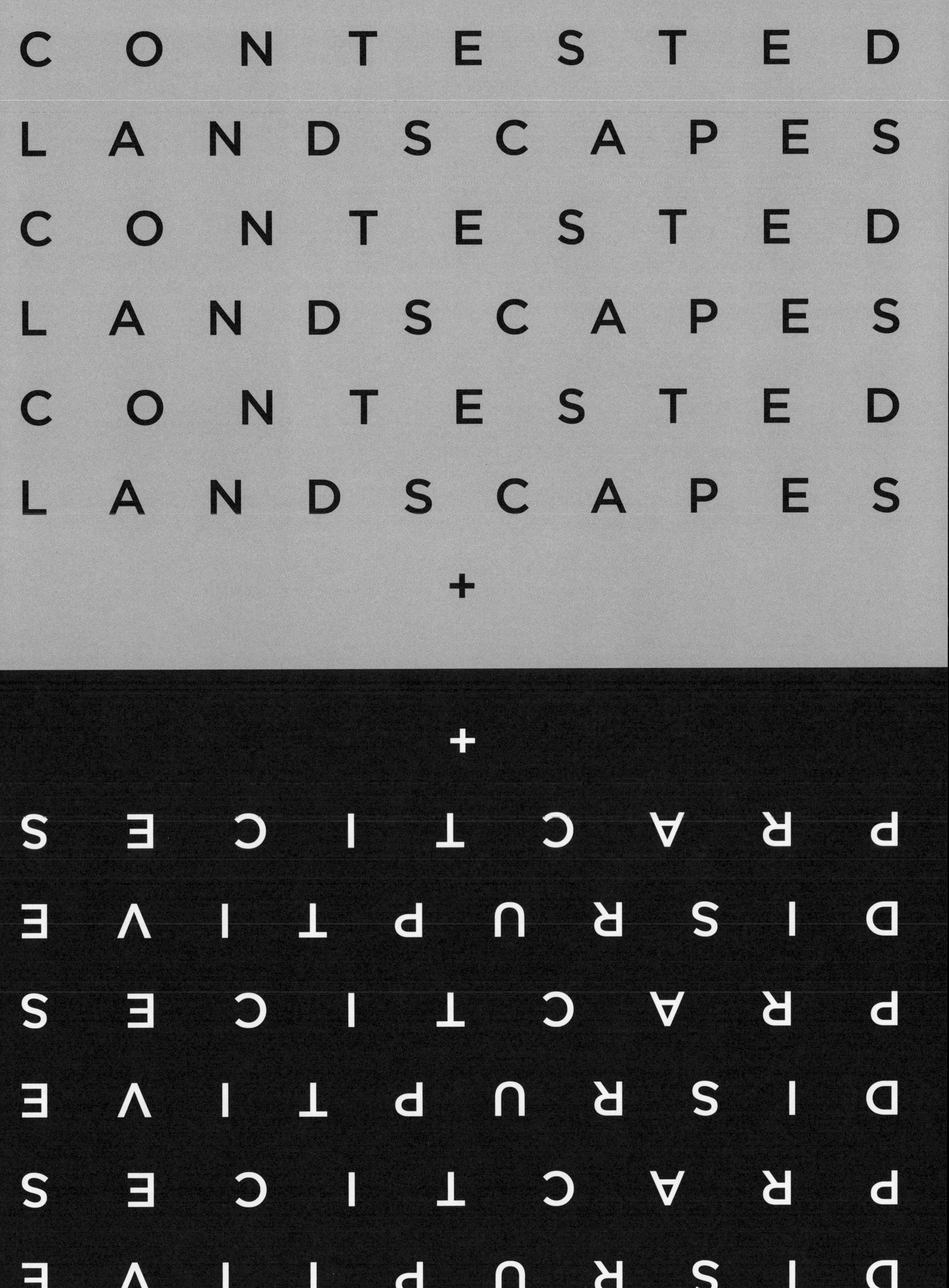
CONTESTED
LANDSCAPES
CONTESTED
LANDSCAPES
CONTESTED
LANDSCAPES
+
+
DISRUPTIVE
PRACTICES
DISRUPTIVE
PRACTICES
DISRUPTIVE
PRACTICES

CONTENTS

CONTESTED

DISRUPTIVE

CONTESTED + DISRUPTIVE

CONTESTED

DISRUPTIVE

Editorial

Nina Middleton
Frances Shuttleworth
Bronwyn Geddes
Jia Jia
Amélie Touboul
Sonja Lutz

Contested Landscapes + Disruptive Practices

In all landscapes, there are elements of tension that challenge and contest our experience. As students of landscape architecture, our awareness is heightened as we are encouraged to provoke and test. We are perplexed by tensions that exist within landscapes. The English Oxford Living Dictionary defines tension as '1. A strained state or condition resulting from forces acting in opposition to each other,' and '2. A relationship between ideas or qualities with conflicting demands or implications.'

We began observing such conditions arising from the competing demands that are placed upon landscapes. The conference Contested Landscapes/ Lost Ecologies, convened by Arctic Frontiers in 2013 at the University of Tromsø, questioned the conflict that is created by extraction processes in the Arctic Circle. The conference argued that 'it [is] necessary to develop a continuous and critical discourse defining, describing and challenging the dynamics and friction between the logics of exploitations and the landscape as a well-balanced ecology.'[1]

We used the conference as a basis for discussion, which provided a framework for this year's theme. To begin, we reiterate a question inspired by the conference: 'are social, political and economical needs compatible with agents and practices that harbour a holistic view on landscape?'[2] In Kerb 25 we wanted to examine the value systems at work in landscapes and the conditions that arise from them. We enquire: are contested landscapes a result of disruptive practices or are disruptive practices a result of contested landscapes?

Michael Murphy explores landscape through the lens of control, understanding that 'the Landscape is formed by processes, such as geology or climate or economics, over which designers exercise little control and, as a consequence, which limit designers' influence over many aspects of the landscape as others might perceive it.'[3] From this, two questions arise. First, how do these processes or competing influences alter and affect landscapes? And second, as a result, how much control do designers really have?

We are presented daily with global events such as war, mass migration and environmental degradation. We found that, no matter their geographical location, everyone is affected by global events in some way. We also found that all landscapes are multi-faceted, comprising of complex living systems. All landscapes experience some form of tension. In presenting our theme Contested Landscapes + Disruptive Practices in Kerb 25 we intend to examine global conflict from a local standpoint.

As Murphy explains, all landscapes are formed and controlled by processes, whether they be social, political, economical, environmental, ecological, geological. Given that we all have observed a degree of contestation in our environments, we looked to the future and wondered how this might affect the practice of landscape architecture within Australia and abroad. With expected population growth, rising energy demands and the inevitable warming of the planet, we wondered how future landscapes would react.

The political climate of 2016 and 2017 was a major talking point. It inspired further questioning of contested landscapes and disruptive practices to grasp how politics, development and culture affect and shape landscapes. From the destruction of Syria and the refugee crisis, the controversy over the North Dakota Pipeline, the resurgence of right wing populism and the introduction of Brexit, and the US election and debate surrounding the US–Mexico border wall, these events all contributed to the framing of Kerb 25.

In exploring the drivers of contestation within landscapes, disruptive practices and conditions, we selected articles for this issue that reflected either a contested landscape, a disruptive practice, or a combination of both. An article that interrogates a contested landscape is 'Geographies of Violence: Island Prisons, Prison Islands, Black Sites' by Suvendrini Perera and Joseph Pugliese. The authors examine intervention in the Middle East and its relationship to the current refugee crisis. Rottnest Island and the imprisonment of First Nation Australians is considered against Manus Island and Nauru, thus questioning the Australian Government's treatment of Indigenous Australians and refugees. Perera and Pugliese frame 'black sites' as island prisons used historically to isolate individuals from society. They observe that the spatial advantages of an island prison lie in its state of control and separation from the mainland, thus creating a contested landscape.

We conceived disruptive practises through two lenses. First, we referred to those practices that created physical disruption, for example extraction processes. Kees Lokman's article 'Wicked Problems Along Canada's Carbon Corridor' explores a physically disruptive practise that contributes to social, environmental and spatial conflict. He examines the resource rich area within British Columbia and Alberta that supports major gas, oil, coal and hydroelectric projects. The level of exploitation within this area is increasing due to demands on energy. Despite this, the area is experiencing vast ecological and spatial transformations, along with demographic conflict and disruption among farming and First Nation communities. Activities such as the practice of resource extraction lead us to question the role of the designer in the future: what new landscapes will we be working with, and how will such landscapes affect the future of design?

Second, we also understand disruptive practices to include those practices that disrupt normative conceptual frameworks or, as Leyla Acaroglu suggests, practices that are 'functionally imbued with the objective of challenging the status quo and making positive change.'[4] RMIT student, Asa Kremmer, who studied at Delft University of Technology, observes in his article the relationship between colonial maps 'as a tool to demarcate walls, fences, checkpoints, and divide people, places and identity.' In 'Atlas of Borders', he outlines how the colonial redrawing of maps saw the displacement of people and entire communities. His article positions a disruptive practice that reduces experiences, culture and connection and proposes a new form of mapping at multiple scales that depicts multidimensional spatial conditions. These themes are evident in other articles in Kerb that similarly highlight how populations are subject to environmental disasters, land loss, climate change and rising sea levels.

Alexandra Mei's project titled 'Rise: A Guide to Boundary Resistance' comprises both a contested landscape and a disruptive practice. Her project examines a watermark on the coastline that is used as a bureaucratic mechanism for state ownership. For the Biloxi-Chitimacha-Choctaw tribe on the Isle de Jean Charles, Louisiana, this line divides native land and state owned water. As water rises over the next 50 years the tribe and many other coastal communities will lose their land. Furthermore, their land has been subdivided by a nearby oil industry and they will have to leave. Mei's project provides tools and methods to reclaim land that holds culture and identity even after they leave. If the mark can be altered and obscured the tribe will remain in ownership of their land.

This project explores the act of boundary making and resistance.

Since Kerb's inception in 1997 it is undeniable that globalisation has allowed for greater numbers of students to access education abroad, and for students to engage with national and international concerns throughout their education. Discussions, articles and projects within this edition of Kerb push the question of 'what is now, what can be and what will be' in the practice and theory of landscape architecture. As students, we are encouraged to be curious, to engage with and examine landscapes, and the complexities that form them. Through Kerb 25 we have recognised that events of 2016/2017 and beyond may affect the practice of landscape architecture in the future. Kerb 25 asks questions and pushes into the unknown. In presenting Contested Landscapes + Disruptive Practices we aim to explore whether the competing demands of the twenty-first century are compatible agents that can foster holistic landscapes. Kerb 25 invites its readers to question whether contested landscapes are a result of disruptive practices, or are disruptive practices a result of contested landscapes?

1. Contested Landscapes – Lost Ecologies / proceedings of the Arctic Frontiers conference, 2013, University of Tromsø, Norway, pp. 1-3 <https://www.arkitektur.no/contested-landscapes-lost-ecologies>

2. Ibid

3. Murphy, M 2016, Landscape Architectural Theory: An Ecological Approach, Island Press, Washington, USA

4. Acaroglu, L 2014, 'Making Change: Explorations into enacting a disruptive pro-sustainability design practice', RMIT University, Melbourne, Australia

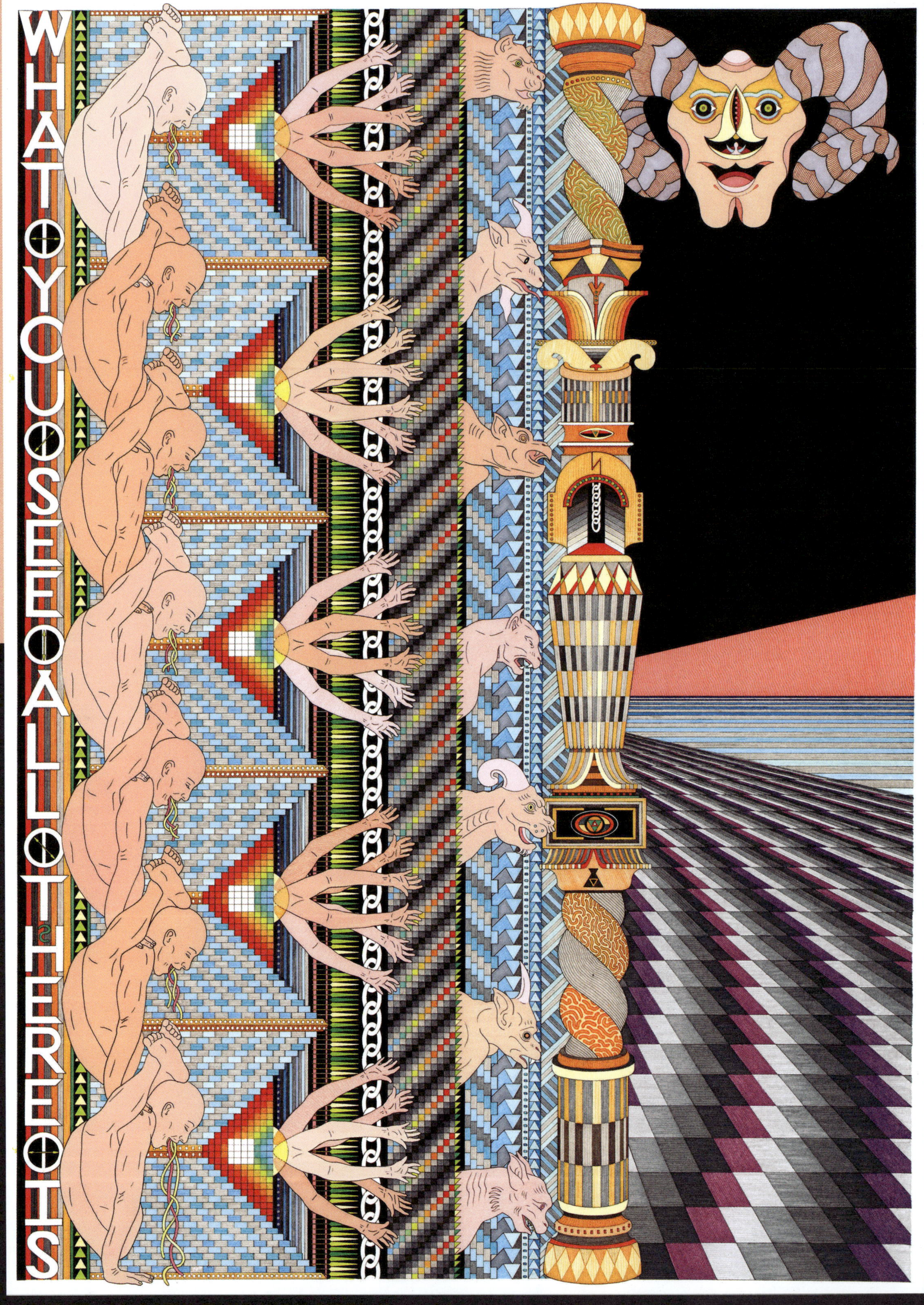
WHAT YOU SEE ALL THERE IS

C O N T E S T E D
C O N T E S T E D
C O N T E S T E D
C O N T E S T E D
C O N T E S T E D
C O N T E S T E D
C O N T E S T E D

C O N T E S T E D
C O N T E S T E D
C O N T E S T E D
C O N T E S T E D
C O N T E S T E D
C O N T E S T E D

Karl Kullman

THINGS THAT MATTER: SHAPING LANDSCAPE AGENCY IN THE ANTHROPOCENE

Divisive landscapes

Straddling diverging tectonic plates, Iceland is tearing apart at a rate of 25 centimetres per century. For nearly a thousand years, annual parliamentary meetings were held amidst this dynamically fissuring landscape.[1] Roughly translating as 'assembly field', *Þingvellir* (Thingvellir) drew Icelanders from across the island for a week to discuss communal matters of concern. Distinctive geomorphic features supported these activities with an assortment of natural hollows and meadows. In the sense that divisive matters of concern were discussed in a literally dividing landscape, the shape of the land influenced cultural practices.

While Þingvellir is the most famous example, landscape parliaments were commonplace throughout Viking territory. As an outdoor venue for discussing important community matters, the Nordic Þing (Thing, assembly) derives from the ancient Germanic proto-parliamentary Ding. As Martin Heidegger observed, this semantic legacy is also retained in the English word 'thing', in the sense that a person 'knows his things'; that is, 'he understands the matters' at hand.[2] But even as Þingvellir's parliament continued to flourish within the uniquely isolated and dynamic landscape of Iceland, 'things' were radically transforming in Continental Europe. With the rise of the centralised state and the application of modern cartography, land enclosure eroded the feudal commons that Thing parliaments typically occupied. With no place left in the landscape, Things moved undercover and eventually into fully enclosed buildings.

Reifying things

As Kenneth Olwig masterfully unpacks, a fundamental transformation occurred for both landscape and things. Where Things were once landscape-based community assemblies for discussing things-that-matter, the architecturalisation of these forums dispossessed Things of their landscape agency. Without agency, things became reified as physical objects, or things-as-matter.[3] Notwithstanding Heidegger's etymological lesson with regards to 'knowing one's things', this is primarily how we conceive of things today: as myriad inanimate and unnamed objects that encircle us with our own indifference.

Landscape also underwent reification. Landscape constituted as a community established through the discussion of things-that-matter transformed into landscape as a spatial aggregation of material things-as-matter.[4] No longer defined from its communal core as a place, the reified landscape became defined more in terms of spatial boundaries for the containment of material things. Fences, walls and the power of pictorial framing shaped this containment. As the focus shifted from substance to scenery, landscape became more of a witness to things than the thing itself.

1. Beck, R 1929, 'Iceland's thousand-year-old parliament', Scandinavian Studies and Notes, vol. 10, no. 5, 149–153; Gudmundsson, A 1987, 'Tectonics of the Thingvellir fissure swarm, SW Iceland', Journal of Structural Geology, vol. 9, no. 1, pp. 61–69;

2. Heidegger, M 1971, 'The thing', in Hofstadter, A (trans.), Poetry Language Thought, Harper & Row, New York, pp. 161–180, p. 173.n

3. Olwig, KR 2013, 'Heidegger, Latour and the reification of things', Geografiska Annaler: Series B, Human Geography, vol. 95, no. 3, pp. 251–273, p. 256.

4. ibid, p. 251.

5. Kullmann, K 2016, 'Route Fittko: tracing Walter Benjamin's path of no return', Ground Up (Delineations), vol. 5, pp. 70–75.

6. Spirn, AW 1984, The Granite Garden: Urban Nature and Human Design, Basic Books, New York, p. 91; Crutzen, PJ 2006, 'The "Anthropocene"', in E Ehlers & T Krafft (eds), Earth System Science in the Anthropocene, Springer, Berlin & Heidelberg, Germany, pp. 13–18.

7. Corner, J 1999, 'Recovering landscape as a critical cultural practice', in J Corner (ed.), Recovering Landscape: Essays in Contemporary Landscape Architecture, Princeton Architectural Press, New York, pp. 1–26.

The landscape of things: Almannagjá gorge at Þingvellir, Iceland.
Image credit: Karl Kullmann

8. Corner, J 1997, 'Ecology and landscape as agents of creativity', in GF Thompson & FR Steiner (eds), Ecological Design and Planning, Wiley, New York, pp. 80–108; Corner, J 1999, 'The agency of mapping: speculation, critique and invention', in D Cosgrove (ed.), Mappings, Reaktion Books, Islington, London, pp. 213–252.

9. Deleuze, G & Guattari , F 1987, A Thousand Plateaus: Capitalism and Schizophrenia, University of Minnesota Press.

10. Livingstone, DN 2010, 'Landscapes of knowledge', in P Meusburger, DN Livingstone & H Jöns (eds.), Geographies of Science, Springer, Berlin, pp. 3-22.

11. Connolly, P 2004, 'Embracing openness: making landscape urbanism landscape architectural: part II', in J Raxworthy & J Blood (eds), The Mesh Book: Landscape Infrastructure, RMIT Press, Melbourne, pp. 206–225.

Contemporary things

Today, even as we submit to a hyperconnected borderless world in which humans and capital move without friction, the landscape is witness to more walls and divisions than ever before.[5] Landscape becomes a scapegoat for the disjunction between the satellite's view of a seamless sphere of mass air travel, instant communications and intercontinental missiles, and the individual's view from the ground where the structures of power are concealed behind closed doors. As the ultimate emblem of ambivalence, things in this reality are relegated to hyper-networked everyday devices within the increasingly expedient Internet of Things.

How might the thingness of the landscape be retrieved from here? It would be naïve to suppose that we could turn back time and relocate the tools of governance back out into the landscape as a kind of recreated Þingvellir. Nor is there any value in physically reconstituting the contemporary landscape-thing as a clichéd local amphitheatre, an empty monument to nostalgia for community gatherings of yore. Since the very nature of gathering has changed, how might the landscape-thing re-emerge to help shape contemporary matters of concern? And what shape might the landscape-thing take?

Geological agents

In essence, these are questions of agency, which has been challenging ground for landscape architecture. On the one hand, humans are 'geological agents' who have assumed a dominant role in shaping the landscape and whose activities are conspicuous within the Quaternary geological record (recently popularised as the Anthropocene).[6] On the other hand, the human geological agent comes burdened with the moral responsibility for stewarding nature that permeates the history of landscape architecture and environmentalism generally.

In a persuasive rewiring of human agency and stewardship, James Corner leveraged landscape agency in the recovery of landscape from a submissive reflection of culture to an active instrument that shapes culture.[7] Privileging process and performance over the landscape traditions of aesthetics and form, ecology and mapping were positioned as key design mechanisms for recovering landscape agency.[8] In co-opting metaphors from A Thousand Plateaus (1987), creative mapping claimed to circumvent the determinism that is often levelled at methodological approaches to environmental design.[9]

While the application of Corner's agency of ecology and mapping barely evolved across the past two decades of design praxis, landscape agency remains intensely contested in wider landscape discourse. As the pendulum swings back and forth between emphasising the influence of society and nature, the anthropic hand restrains landscape agency.[10] Even Corner's widely adopted strategies of indeterminacy, emergence, scaffoldings and creative mapping - which aim to divest the traditional master-planner's oversight - ultimately defer to an external human designer to pull the levers of selectivity that set these processes in motion.[11]

Assembling things

Set within the existential ecological crises of the Anthropocene, Bruno Latour extends agency beyond humans and the landscapes that they instigate. No longer external entities awaiting human activation, non-human objects become as empowered to instigate actions as their human counterparts. By emphasising their interconnections, he situates humans and non-human actors symmetrically, with actions arising from their collective pursuits.[12]

Latour applies these symmetrical actor-networks to an object-oriented politics encompassing the many issues to which humans are connected. Typically overlooked as 'matters-of-fact' that are incidental to political forums, objects are recast as 'matters-of-concern' that are as important as the actual topics up for discussion.[13] Following Heidegger, objects are thus assembled as gatherings - or things - that draw issues together. In support of this politics of things, Latour observes that ancient Things comprised not only people but also were thick with other things, ranging from garments to structures, cities and complex technologies to facilitate gathering.

Latour concedes, however, that because the 'shape' of contemporary assemblies has changed we cannot simply go back to old Things. Clearly, political forums, historically moving from landscape to architecture, drive this shape-shift. But it is not simply a question of designing larger and more elaborate arenas within which to assemble, since at the end of the day it is our political horizons that are too limited to address the global scope of the Anthropocene.

Inflecting things

Latour calls on designers to find and represent the shape of thing-assemblies in the Anthropocene. Since 'scape' is

12. Latour, B 2005, Reassembling the social: an introduction to actor-network-theory, Oxford University Press, UK.

13. Latour, B 2005, 'From realpolitik to dingpolitik or how to make things public', in B Latour & P Weibel (eds), Making Things Public: Atmospheres of Democracy, MIT Press, Cambridge MA, pp. 4–31, p. 9.

14. Scape derives from the Dutch suffix *schap*, which, like the German suffix *schaft*, means shape; Edward CS 2002, Representing Place: Landscape Painting and Maps, University of Minnesota Press.

15. Kullmann, K 2016, 'Concave worlds, artificial horizons: reframing the urban public garden', Studies in the History of Gardens and Designed Landscapes, vol. 37, no. 1, pp. 15–32.

16. De Landa, M 1997, A Thousand Years of Nonlinear History, Zone Books, New York.

17. Morton, T 2013, Hyperobjects: Philosophy and Ecology after the End of the World, University of Minnesota Press.

18. Latour, B 2008, 'A cautious

Fluid geographies: The Öxará River intercepting the Þingvellir Fissure Swarm.
Image credit: Karl Kullmann

etymologically 'shape', this challenge resonates with landscape architecture.[14] The agency of the land-shape is emphatically illustrated at Þingvellir, where the unique geomorphology nurtured the development of cultural practices. And although the distinctive land-shapes cleaved by dividing tectonic plates are unique to Iceland, elsewhere in the Viking world Things inhabited similarly scoured shapes of post-glacial landscapes. Both geomorphologies create topographies that gather matters-of-concern within their irregular inflections and folds.

Without being deterministic, it is significant that landscape parliaments thrived for far longer in these amorphous Nordic landscapes than in the more typical dendritic landscapes of Continental Europe. The converging flows of dendritic river systems support central control from a maritime or riverine location, with tendrils of power extending upstream into the hinterlands. Here, water becomes an allegory for time, which privileges the inexorable flow of modern progress and the convergence of history.[15] In juxtaposition, the inflections of post-glacial and tectonic-rift terrain invoke a more temporally variable sense of landscape. This temporal variability explicates the privileging of space over time in the chronicling of the Icelandic Sagas across a thousand years of non-linear history.[16] Indeed, temporal variability applies to the very idea of landscape, which, unlike architecture and the other arts generally, precedes and succeeds the landscape architect and their tools.

So, although we cannot reverse time in the sense of returning to ancient Things, we can perceive contemporary things as landscape inflections in place of rigidly enclosed sites. The landscape inflection functions like a semipermeable threshold, in the sense that it balances openness and enclosure. Too much openness and the landscape-thing is vulnerable to dissipation into the background noise of myriad other things. Too much containment and the landscape-thing risks suffocation from the limitations placed on access and participation. The variable temporality of the landscape inflection extends matters-of-concern beyond our preoccupation with our own present and immediate futures, which, from ecological crises to genetic design, encompass vast and miniscule scales and temporalities.[17]

Drawing things

With regards to the challenge of representing the ambiguous and controversial nature of matters-of-concern, Latour cites the limitations of centuries of innovation in visualisation techniques and technologies. From perspectival projection to CAD, we have mastered the art of drawing objects but remain unable to satisfactorily draw together, approximate or model the complexity of things.[18] With ongoing aspirations for communicating the conceptual essence of the nuanced landscape instead of merely simulating its physical attributes, the history of landscape architectural visualisation mirrors this representational struggle.[19]

The inadequacy of techniques that represent the shape of things is largely a consequence of things being entangled with myriad other things. With a remit for locating physical features of the earth's topos (place), landscape architecture's go-to medium of topography struggles to permeate this thickened landscape. From high in the sky, the Cartesian/satellite basis of topography fuses things together into a superficial surface that dilutes the distinctive shape of each thing. And as intoxicating as it may be, the capacity to zoom in and out with impunity in Google Earth, GIS or CAD remains an optical illusion; even as the satellite oversees everything from orbit, it overlooks the nuances of the topos.

Novel representation techniques that retain the distinctiveness of interconnected things may draw insight from the archaic mapping practice of chorography. The remit of chorography is the local region, where the representation of landscape elements is prioritised over Cartesian precision. In contrast to the aloof gaze of Cartesian mapping, chorography places the mapper within the field of survey, and often within the map itself. Instead of zooming in and out, as in frictionless Cartesian space, chorographic space stretches and sticks to all of the things that coagulate around matters-of-concern. And if the satellite's geostationary orbit came to symbolise the technological apotheosis of Cartesian mapping, the drone's wandering eye becomes a technological symbol of thing-chorography, as it permeates things amidst the thickened topo-spheric zone.[20]

Prometheus? A few steps toward a philosophy of design (with special attention to Peter Sloterdijk)', Keynote lecture for the Networks of Design meeting of the Design History Society, Falmouth, Cornwall.

19. Kullmann, K 2014, 'Hyper-realism and loose-reality: the limitations of digital realism and alternative principles in landscape design visualization', Journal of Landscape Architecture, vol. 9, no. 3, pp. 20–31.

20. Kullmann, K 2017, 'The satellite's progeny: digital chorography in the age of drone vision', Forty-Five: Journal of Outside Research, no. 157, <http://forty-five.com/papers/157>.

21. Latour, B 2014, 'Agency at the time of the Anthropocene', New Literary History, vol. 45, pp. 1–18, p. 17; Latour, B 2004, 'From "matters of facts" to "states of affairs": which protocol for the new collective experiments?', in H Schmidgen, P Geimer & S Dierig (eds), Experimental Cultures, Kulturverlag Kadmos, Berlin, <http://www.bruno-latour.fr/node/372>.

22. Kullmann, K 2017, 'The garden of entangled paths: landscape phenomena at the Albany Bulb wasteland', Landscape Review, vol. 17, no. 1, pp. 58–77.

23. ibid., 16.

24. Kullmann, K 2015, 'The usefulness of uselessness: towards a landscape framework for un-activated urban public space', Architectural Theory Review, vol. 19, no. 2, pp. 154–173.

Cultivating things

Latour connects drawing to its etymological cognate, design. If design is drawing together, and if Things are gatherings, things are created through collaborative design. For Latour, collaborative design is always redesign in the sense that some issue or problem exists first. And although the value of collaborative design has long been established within landscape architecture, the stakeholders are typically human. In Latour's collective experiment in a public laboratory, all agents - human and non-human - shape the process, even if they are not always apparent, included or willing.[21]

But while the collective experiment is appealing in theory, the means by which non-human collaborators express agency remains ambiguous. Letting non-humans speak invokes a type of animism, whereby animals, plants, rocks and wind express life forces independent of human enablement. The process through which the landscape architect participates within collaborations is also uncertain. When all actors are granted equal status, the role and skills of the designer are ultimately no more substantial than the opinion of a pebble.

Reconceptualising the designer as a type of gardener embedded within collective experiments clarifies the role of the landscape architect in things. In one of the most immersive roles a human can undertake in their environment, a gardener digs, cultivates, gathers, propagates, grafts, shapes, amplifies and rearranges things in a garden. As the garden reveals its agency over time, the gardener continually amends and adapts their designs.[22] As a designer-gardener, the landscape architect is part participant, through deep involvement in the ecological and social processes that shape a particular issue or project. They are part experimenter, as they balance participation with the need to let processes take their course, even without the immediate endorsement of all (human and non-human) actors. And they are part steward, since they are not ignorant or indifferent to many of the potential outcomes that the levers of design may unfurl into the landscape.

Hybridising things

Latour observes that Things are no longer limited to conventional parliaments but extend to many other hybrid assemblages; supermarkets, financial markets, hospitals and computer networks become forums for matters-of-concern.[23] Landscape architecture is well versed in hybrid forms, since landscape in all its messy complexity is rarely unalloyed to something else. The re-envisioning of landscape as infrastructure is one such assemblage that hybridises the performance aspects of the working landscape with the cultural landscape of urbanism. A park is no longer an isolated island puncturing the flux of the metropolis, but is hardwired into a larger landscape system, which, like digital infrastructure, may be invisible to the casual observer.

On the whole, however, the designed landscape remains true to type. We know what to expect and how to behave in a pocket park versus a city square versus a wilderness preserve. And although conforming to type maximises legibility, performance and accountability, it constrains the capacity of landscape to stretch into shapes that cultivate novel gatherings. With the dissolution of clear distinctions between nature and culture in the Anthropocene, a landscape-of-things demands more radical recompositions of landscape types into novel hybrid assemblages.

Perhaps the semipermeable threshold that traditionally frames the garden could be hybridised with the contested public realm of the street. In its conventional role as an access and utilities corridor, the street is still occasionally a setting for community participation, in the sense that people who are gathered around a matter-of-concern 'take to the streets'. The tactically integrated semipermeable threshold might help focus the mob, which, in the United States at least, often ends up on the freeway before dissipating into a haze of capsicum spray and unfulfilled aspirations. It may also achieve nothing of the sort; just like biological hybridisation, a hybrid-type may fail to become a landscape-thing. But given that landscape and human actors are both remarkably adept at adapting and adopting sites and subcultures in unforeseen ways, it is bound to become something.[24] After all, the landscape always remains present; it inherently matters.

Cultivating things: the immersed designer as gardener, who is part steward, part experimenter and part participant. Image by Mark Tansey, Robbe-Grillet Cleansing Every Object in Sight, 1981.

Oil on canvas with crayon, 182.9 x 183.4 cm, Gift of Mr. and Mrs. Warren Brandt, © 2017 Mark Tansey, DIGITAL IMAGE © 2017, The Museum of Modern Art/ Scala, Florence.

Emma
Mendel

MODELLING RECIPROCITY: BLURRING EDGES BETWEEN DEFINITIONS

The industrial era allowed for efficiencies in water safety, food and transportation but in turn left severed the agrarian era's linkages between function and living. As we progress into a shared economy, we begin to strengthen these mutable boundaries. Modelling reciprocity stems from the political reconciliation disclosures between First Nations and Canada through the elucidation of gradients between edges of materials.

In the Anishinaabe community, water is seen as a living force and the centre of life rather than simply a component of it. By understanding the relationships and histories that Anishinaabe communities have with their land, these models explore landscape perception and representation. Rejecting conventional mapping techniques that believe a hard line separates land from water, these representations and models take a moment to dilate the reciprocal relationships between the two. By drawing with water, time, sedimentation and evaporation, traces of what happened to the materials are left behind, articulating land as water and water as land. These models created a design process that generates a visual language to communicate what water means to the Anishinaabe culture.

Suvendrini Perera & Joseph Pugliese

:

GEOGRAPHIES OF VIOLENCE: ISLAND PRISONS, PRISON ISLANDS, BLACK SITES

Australia, the sometime-island-prison, which proclaims itself as a geographical exception, the island continent, is defined by the figure of the island as prison.[1] In the drawing, One Asylum Seeker in Nauru, the artist and poet Ravi, a former inmate, powerfully represents the sense of disabling immobilisation and isolation experienced by those Australia imprisons offshore in its camps on Nauru and Manus Island, encaging them in a mesh of restrictions that are at once spatial, legal and physical.

Following a trip to Australia's Christmas Island Detention Centre in 2008, Pamela Curr, Coordinator of the Asylum Seeker Resource Centre, told a reporter, 'The leitmotif is cage – all sizes and shapes. Everything is caged, lights, gym, cameras everything.'[2] Cages within cages, prisons within prisons, islands within islands: these are enduring features of the Australian state's territorialising practices, the defining contours of its past and present. These territorialising practices organise spatial, geographic and environmental factors so as to reinforce Australia's self-definition as a state that is racially and culturally distinct and separate from the region, and whose insular status needs to be preserved by an ensemble of legal and extralegal measures. A shifting geography of land and sea, of fortified beaches and coastlines, of weaponised oceans, whose natural dangers are intensified by official 'deterrence' policies that push asylum seekers into ever more risky ventures, of penal camps and island prisons: this is the carceral landscape whose outlines we sketch in what follows.

Australia's history of colonial violence against Indigenous peoples can be mapped through a geography of island prisons, from jails and internment camps (Rottnest Island) to reserves (Palm Island) and lock hospitals (Bernier and Dorre Islands). These are the antecedents of present day island camps for refugees, designed as the very antithesis of shelter. All these sites function to instil a sense of dislocation and isolation, where even the surrounding landscape compounds the suffering of the prisoners, as the vision of an island paradise proves so at odds with their circumstances. In her memoir, Born a Half Caste, Marnie Kennedy, a Kalkadoon woman who was removed to Palm Island as a child, recounts:

> When I first went to Palm Island I can remember it was on a cargo boat, and I can remember screaming while being loaded into a small boat ...The settlement was just being started. ... We lived in a huge grass dormitory, mostly mothers with their children ... The men who had wives

1. Perera, S 2009, Australia and the Insular Imagination: Beaches, Borders, Boats and Bodies, Palgrave Macmillan, New York.

2. Black, S 2008, 'Inside the Christmas Island Detention Centre', Crikey, <http://www.crikey.com.au/2008/08/19/inside-the-christmas-island-detention-centre/>.

3. Kennedy, M 1990, Born a Half-Caste, Aboriginal Studies Press, Canberra, ACT.

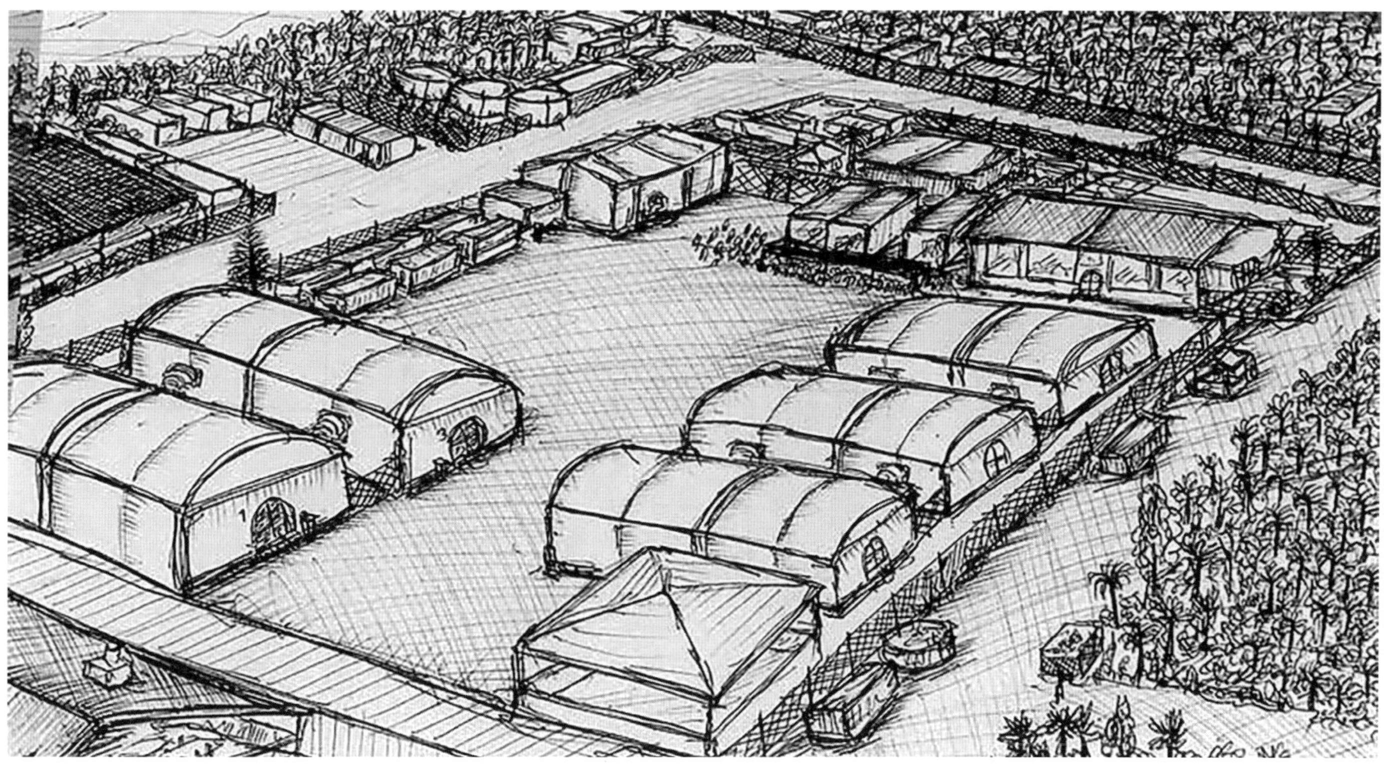

'Manus Detention Camp'
©Eaten Fish, Reproduced with the permission of the artist.

> lived in their grass houses called the camps. There may have been two to three hundred people. Palm Island lies forty miles east of Townsville. It was one of the most beautiful islands. As the ships steamed through the channels to anchor outside the reef you would see the mountains with the clouds scudding across them and on fine days you would see the island a mass of green and yellow. With the wattle trees in full bloom, their perfume would float down over the island ... There was an aura about this island. Something so beautiful it held you in awe. It is hard to believe that this beautiful island was a penal settlement. This island was meant for romance, love and to live happily ever after.[3]

Kennedy's memories find a striking echo in the narratives of asylum seekers held on Nauru and Manus Island. The award-winning drawings of Eaten Fish, the Iranian artist imprisoned on Manus Island, frequently highlight the dissonance between the postcard beauty of the Pacific island setting and the mental and physical abuse to which detainees held there are subjected.[4] Similarly, Pari, a young Iranian woman, who with her husband, Omid, sought asylum in Australia, recounts how the beautiful sunsets on Nauru were a source of grief and pain to the detainees who, like Kennedy in her very different prison, were reminded every day of the unbridgeable distance between their reality and the vision of the island as a place of romantic beauty: 'People often cried while watching the sun go down ... Every sunset was a symbol of another day lost'.[5]

In these accounts of incarceration on Palm Island and Nauru, separated by several decades, both the beauty and the terror of the natural environment are mobilised to increase the sufferings of those imprisoned there, adding to their sense of agonising isolation and the consciousness of being cast away. Despite the odds, Pari and Omid tried to hold fast to the sunset as the promise of another day and to the dream of the island as a place 'meant for romance, love and to live happily ever after.' Their hopes were cruelly shattered one morning when Omid set fire to himself in an effort to convince an international delegation of their desperate plight. Fatal delays in airlifting his seriously injured body to Australia resulted in his agonised death. Pari, though a recognised refugee, remains in detention in Brisbane devastated with loss and grief, with no prospect of release:

> Every day since, Pari has been held in isolated detention in Australia: alone, traumatised, segregated

and trapped in a Kafkaesque legal and political nightmare. She has not seen a sunset since, and faces an indefinite incarceration, despite being formally recognised as a refugee who fled persecution and who is legally owed protection.[6]

Fearful insularities, violent sovereignties

Australia's establishment as a settler state in 1901 was preceded by the geographical and racial consolidation of the new nation as an island of whiteness surrounded by the alien and amorphous nonwhite geographies of Asia and the Pacific. As it cast itself off from the surrounding seas, coastlines and archipelagos by designating itself as an island, separate, self-contained and white, Australia exercised its fearful and violent sovereignty both internally, by dispossessing the original inhabitants from their land through policies of displacement and deterritorialisation, and externally, by adopting a stance of imperial mastery over the region. Current practices of establishing places of detention in neighbouring territories exist on a continuum with these imperial and racial assertions of territorial and racial sovereignty over the region. They are practices that, as Anthony Burke puts it, cast security as a founding axiom of the Australian state, 'a political technology' that structures its institutions, sites, and subjectivities, 'at once produc[ing] and manipulat[ing] bodies, identities, societies, spaces and flows'.[7]

According to a report published in mid-2008, Australia 'claims rights over more waters than any other nation' with 'sovereignty interests embracing parts of the Pacific, Indian and Southern Oceans, and the Tasman, Coral, Timor and Arafura seas'; further, it claims to exercise 'some form of sovereign right' over external territories amounting to 10.7 million square kilometres, an area greater than the external territorial claims of the United States.[8] These vast territorial interests were amassed through a series of tough negotiations in the period of decolonisation, playing on the needs and desires of newly-independent states such as Papua New Guinea and Indonesia, as well as on the anxieties of their departing imperial masters. Sovereignty over Christmas Island, previously controlled via Singapore, was transferred to Australia by Britain in 1957 to 'keep the island's phosphate reserves and strategically useful airfields in safe hands'.[9] Britain handed the Cocos (Keeling) Islands, to Australia two years earlier in 1955. Both Christmas and Cocos Islands, as Indian Ocean islands largely populated by non-white indentured labour imported in the colonial period, remain extraneous to Australia, although officially part of it. Significantly, these would be the first Australian territories to be excised from the migration zone when they became landing points for people seeking asylum.

The unexpected consequence of Australia's policies of territorial aggrandisement, as Hamish McDonald drily points out, is that the successful expansion of its maritime possessions paradoxically brought with it, not a sense of security, but its opposite: persistent anxieties over intruders in this newly acquired sovereign zone. Fishing craft from the Indonesian island of Rote seeking to ply their traditional waters, germs and alien infections migrating across the lines in the sea, refugees seeking asylum on its outlying territories: all trigger a gamut of racially charged fears from infection to infiltration.[10]

Since the arrival of the first ramshackle boats crowded with refugees from the war in Vietnam and its aftermath, asylum seekers have sought to thread their way through the Southeast Asian archipelago to make landfall on outcrops of Australian territory or even on some mainland beach. The policy of compulsorily imprisoning asylum seekers who arrive by boat, but not those who seek asylum at airports after arriving by plane, was initiated by a Labor government in 1992. It was extended to levels of unimaginable systemic violence by a Liberal-National coalition government in succeeding years.[11][12] Political frenzies over defending Australia from arrivals by sea were nourished and stoked through a multiplicity of territorial practices since 2001. These included the excision of parts of the mainland from the migration zone with, in some cases, retrospective denials applied to asylum seekers who had already made landfall on Australian soil; it culminated in the excision of the entire territorial landmass of Australia from its own migration zone.[13] At the same time, programs of covert disruption to prevent boats from setting

4. Perera, S & Pugliese, J 2016, 'A nightmare world in plain sight: the artworks of Mr Eaten Fish', Researchers Against Pacific Black Sites, <http://researchersagainstpacificblacksites.org/index.php/2016/07/15/a-nightmare-world-in-plain-sight/>.

5. Doherty, B 2017, 'Death in detention: "I'd give everything to have him back"', The Guardian, <https://www.theguardian.com/australia-news/2017/mar/23/death-in-detention-id-give-everything-to-have-him-back>.

6. Ibid 5, p. 2.

7. Burke, A 2001, Fear of Security: Australia's Invasion Anxiety, Cambridge University Press, Cambridge.

8. Woolner, D 2008, 'Strategic insights - policing our ocean domain: establishing an Australian Coast Guard', Australian Strategic Policy Institute, <https://www.aspi.org.au/publications/strategic-insights-41-policing-our-ocean-domain-establishing-an-australian-coast-guard/SI41_Coastguard.pdf>.

9. McDonald, H 2009, 'We took a lot and now we have a lot to give', Sydney Morning Herald, 25 April 2017.

10. Balint, R 2005, Troubled waters: borders, boundaries and possession in the Timor Sea, Allen & Unwin, Crows Nest, NSW.

11. Pugliese, J 2002, 'Penal Asylum: Refugees, Ethics, Hospitality,' Borderlands, vol. 1, no. 1, <http://www.borderlands.net.au/vol1no1_2002/pugliese.html>.

12. Pugliese, J 2003, 'Each death is the first death', Heat, Vol. 6, pp. 7-12.

13. Perera, S 2015, 'Burning our boats', Journal of the Association for the Study of Australian Literature, <http://openjournals.library.usyd.edu.au/index.php/JASAL/article/viewFile/10560/10438>.

sail or arriving, legal sleights of hand ('enhanced screening'), deportations, and enforced boat turn backs further attempted to deter boat arrivals.

These practices of violent territoriality found their most extreme expression to date in the uncompromisingly titled Operation Sovereign Borders, put into effect in late 2013, under a joint military-political command. This relentless operation combined boat turnbacks, operating under a veil of secrecy over 'on-water matters' with the grimly titled No Advantage Policy. The latter provides the core principles for the second phase of the Pacific Solution. This is the policy under which Ravi, Omid and Pari, the three recognised refugees cited above, as well as close to 2000 others, have been incarcerated in island prisons on Nauru, Manus Island, Christmas Island and elsewhere. Several thousand more children, women and men are in on-shore detention or subject to other indefinite sentences in the limbo of 'temporary protection'.

Offshore detention and the black site

As outsourced enclaves, located outside Australian borders on its former colonial protectorates of Nauru and Papua New Guinea, offshore detention camps are pitched on shaky legal ground, in a shifting territoriality somewhere between Australia and the impoverished client states that act as its overseers and landlords.[14] An ever-changing cast of multinational companies - most recently G4S, Transfield and Broadspectrum - are contracted to operate them. Despite the nominal responsibility of the Nauru and PNG governments, all major decisions for these camps are referred to the Australian Department of Immigration and Border Protection (DIBP). The neocolonial nature of this arrangement is underlined by the fact that Australian citizens are employed in managerial and supervisory roles throughout the camps, with quotas of local PNG and Nauru staff contracted for mostly menial roles, such as cleaners and guards. The ethno-racial, religious and national tensions that this arrangement inevitably engenders among expatriates, locals and inmates adds a further dimension to the structure of displacement.

The convoluted spatio-legal architecture of the offshore camps functions to obfuscate sovereign responsibility and endlessly defer accountability under law for the plight of the inmates, the overwhelming majority of whom are recognised refugees. In our attempts to theorise the structure of these offshore detention camps we have drawn on the concept of 'black sites'.[15] The term 'black sites' has been widely used in the war on terror to describe locations where the US and its allies maintain secret prisons or conduct other illicit activities away from public or legal scrutiny.[16] These sites are characterised by secrecy and lack of accountability. They are most often located in racialised and/or formerly colonised territories, and they continue practices of abuse and torture perpetrated there against colonised peoples. We refer to Australia's camps on its own former colonial territories of Manus Island, PNG, and Nauru as black sites in order to highlight their structural connections with other extra-legal or illegal places of confinement, abuse and torture. Our use of the term 'black site' highlights the linkages between Australia's racialised imprisonment of refugees and the geopolitics of the war on terror within which Australia's Pacific Solution must be located.

Arrested lives

As we have discussed in detail elsewhere, Australia's black sites in Nauru and Papua New Guinea are characterised by 'an architecture that is the very antithesis of shelter: they are spaces designed to engender fear, compound uncertainty and maximise a sense of exposure to danger'.[17] This remains the case despite a ruling by the PNG High Court in April 2016 and an earlier decision by the Nauru government in October 2015, both officially decreeing that the camp inmates were not prisoners.[18][19] Although they may be no longer forcibly confined, Australia's detainees remain unfree, in a state of insufferable uncertainty, compounded by daily fear of violence.[20] Their reality is that of a prison within a prison, perversely, within which the brute physical structures of the camp - its barbed wire fences, quarantine compounds and confinement cells - at times represent a form of protection against the dangers of the surrounding towns and villages where xenophobic resentment and epidemic levels of rape, beatings and other forms of violence

14. Giannacopulos, M 2016, 'Does Exposing State Violence End It?', Overland, 29 September, <https://overland.org.au/2016/09/does-exposing-state-violence-end-it/>.

15. Perera, S & Pugliese, J 2015, 'Offshore Black Sites Open the Door to Torture', The Conversation, <https://theconversation.com/offshore-detention-black-sites-open-door-to-torture-46400>.

16. Pugliese, J 2013, 'State violence and the execution of law: biopolitical caesurae of torture, black sites', drones, Routledge, Abingdon, NY and New York, pp. 161-83.

17. Perera, S & Pugliese, J 2016, '"Anti-Shelter", Insecurities: tracing displacement and shelter', MoMA, <https://medium.com/insecurities/anti-shelter-55842842d4e3#.d8wdihulu>.

18. Tlozek, E & Anderson, S 2016, 'PNG's Supreme Court rules detention of asylum seekers on Manus Island is illegal', ABC News, 27 April, <http://www.abc.net.au/news/2016-04-26/png-court-rules-asylum-seeker-detention-manus-island-illegal/7360078>.

19. Henderson, A & Anderson, S 2015, 'Nauru to process all asylum seekers in offshore detention centre "within the next week"; refugees among those to assess applications', ABC News, 5 October, <http://www.abc.net.au/news/2015-10-05/asylum-seekers-on-nauru-to-be-processed-within-the-next-week/6828130>.

20. Perera, S & Pugliese, J 2015, 'Detainees on Nauru may have been "released", but they are not free', The Conversation, <https://theconversation.com/detainees-on-nauru-may-have-been-released-but-they-are-not-free-48648>.

21. Harvey, G 2017, 'Australia's two faces on violence against women', Asylum Insight, <http://www.asyluminsight.com/c-gemima-harvey/?rq=gemima#.WRJr21JL06j>.

against refugees prevail.[21][22] Most recently, on Good Friday, April 2017, members of the PNG Navy attacked the camp while refugees covered in terror, in fear of another incursion such as the one in which Reza Bharati was killed in 2014.[23] Attempted suicide and self-harm have become all too common responses to this experience of anti-asylum without hope of parole or escape.

The Good Friday attack on Manus camps followed a finding by Papua New Guinea's Chief Justice, Sir Salamo Injia, in which the Manus Island detention centre was declared to be formally closed.[24] The finding was compelled by the previous PNG Supreme Court decision that found the detention centre to be illegal because it breached PNG's constitution.[25] But despite the juridical declaration, nothing has changed, except in name, for the refugees and asylum seekers detained there. They have been told that they no longer inhabit a detention centre, even though they have not been moved from their existing compounds; rather, the detention centre has now reverted to its original military purpose, a naval base, while still effectively functioning as a detention centre. A certain brutal and circular logic here fulfils itself: a naval base becomes a detention centre that, in turn, reverts back to a military facility.

In the space between these two forms of law, the men of Manus detention centre fall through: to nowhere. In the locus of this nowhere, their lives are arrested. The refugees and asylum seekers of Manus, like those on Nauru, continue to lead arrested lives: arrested on arrival by boat to Australia's excised immigration zones and dispatched to offshore immigration prisons. Arrested in the annihilating space of indefinite detention, where there is no time, and where everything is held in a state of suffocating and oppressive suspension. Arrested into a state of paralysing immobility in which there is no glimpsing of a future. Arrested in a space where they have been converted into commodities of exchange in a dubious deal with the United States that has, thus far, delivered them no exit from their detention or suffering.

22. Zable, A 2015, 'Iranian journalist Behrouz Boochani tells of the horrors of Manus Island: out of sight, out of mind', Sydney Morning Herald, <http://www.smh.com.au/comment/iranian-journalist-behrouz-boochani-tells-of-the-horrors-of-manus-island-out-of-sight-out-of-mind-20150921-gjrdi8.html>.

23. Wroe, D & Whyte, S 2014, 'Reza Barati: Two men arrested over death of asylum seeker at PNG detention centre', Sydney Morning Herald, <http://www.smh.com.au/federal-politics/political-news/reza-barati-two-men-arrested-over-death-of-asylum-seeker-at-png-detention-centre-20140819-3dyf3.html>.

24. Tlozek, E 2017, 'PNG Chief Justice finds Manus Island detention centre is actually closed', ABC News, <http://www.abc.net.au/news/2017-03-13/png-chief-justice-finds-manus-island-detention-centre-closed/8350600>.

25. Ibid 18.

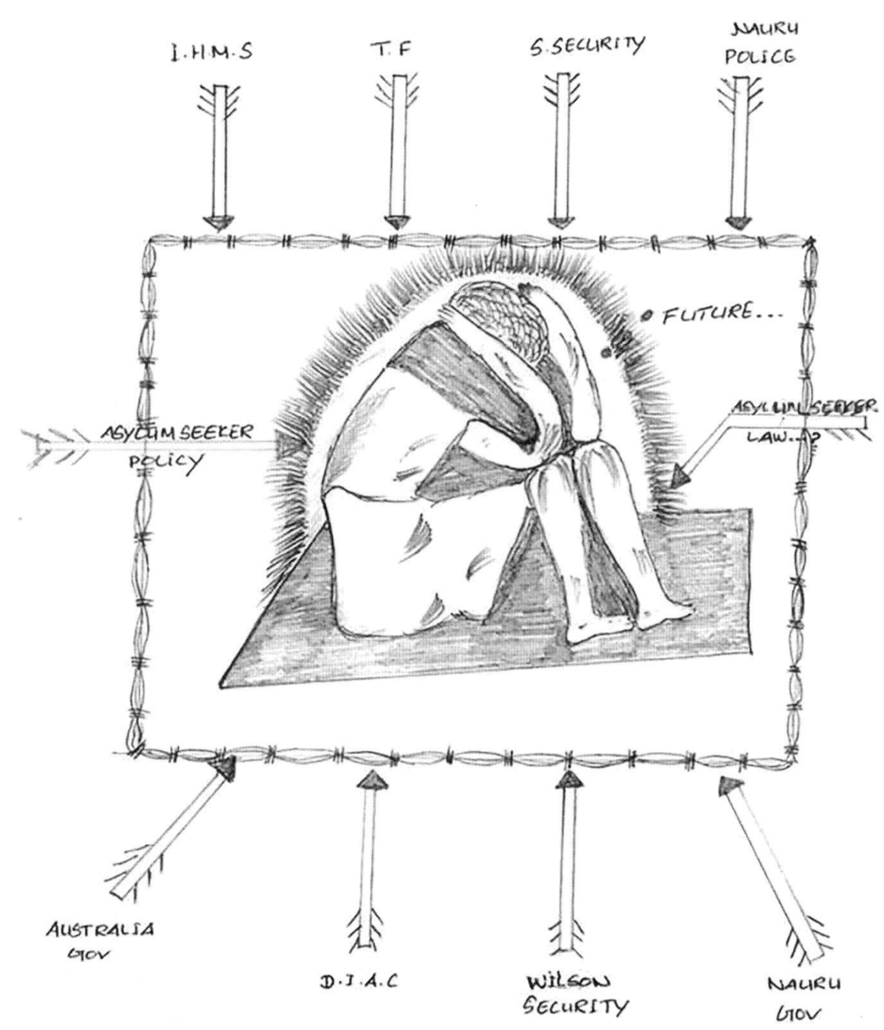

'One Asylum Seeker in Nauru' © Ravi. Reproduced with the permission of the artist.

Shuang Shuang Wu

AMERICAN LANDSCAPE ON BORDER

Shuang Wu's project American Landscape on Border is interested in the influence of politics and large-scale political infrastructure on social and natural landscapes along the Mexico-United States border. The Mexico-United States border has one of the largest cross-border income gaps in the world, and Wu identifies immediate economic and social impacts resulting from this gap as deeply imbedded within the spatially separated landscape.[1] To survey this, particular attention is given to documenting the built environment of the border as a representation of identity, and observing how this landscape is responsive to a dynamic social and cultural relationship. American Landscape on Border identifies major infrastructures related to border crossing activities. Despite the construction of a physical separation system consisting of barriers and fences, regional residents engage in border crossing as a normal activity of everyday life.

1. Anderson, JB & Gerber, J 2008, Fifty Years of Changes on the US – Mexico Border: Growth, Development, and Quality of Life, University of Texas Press, Austin.

BORDER TAXI

Judge

205

Anywhere
For
25¢
Local
25¢
USA
25¢
Mexico

BORDER TAXI

SASABE
STORE

ECTOPLASMIC
MYSTAGOGUE

DISRUPTIVE
DISRUPTIVE
DISRUPTIVE
DISRUPTIVE
DISRUPTIVE
DISRUPTIVE
DISRUPTIVE

Gean Moreno &
Ernesto Oroza

NOTES ON THE MOIRE HOUSE: URBANISM FOR EMPTYING CITIES

1.
Density and congestion have been urbanism's greatest problems in the past few decades. The demographic explosions of the new megalopolis strain the conceptual tools of the discipline, the scope at which it usually works, and the orderly patterns that give it a solid foothold. Urbanism may have recently been surprised by a recurrent but low-key problem that has taken on new dimensions, a problem that is the very opposite of what the field may have thought its coming challenges would be: a potential demographic emptying of cities due to the recent housing crises and the waves of foreclosures, evictions and business shutdowns that they have unleashed. Certain cities are on the verge of becoming vacant. Detroit is, of course, the paradigmatic case. Andrea Branzi has spoken of an above-ground empty doppelgänger of Tokyo, comprised of the over two million square metres of unused office space in that city.[1] Various neighbourhoods in Miami, our theatre of operations, are halfway to becoming ghost towns. Blocks and blocks of single-family houses are boarded up. Entire condo towers are empty. Once bustling business areas are growing idle. Emptying cities put new demands on urbanism.

2.
When neither time nor the resources for long-term strategies are available, one has to start thinking less in terms of implementation than suspension, less of rewriting codes than clearing paths. One has to ride available waves (new or previously undervalued behavioural patterns), find loopholes, disregard protocols, disempower bureaucracies and loosen demands. If this has to do with urbanism at all, it is tactical and aleatory. It would be an urbanism, like Michel de Certeau's 'tactics', that involves actions and modes of behaviour that function without relying on a legitimising institution.[2] It would merely employ, opportunistically, the ground that official practices produce as temporary support structures from where to unleash unexpected performative elements. (Tactics here are efforts to find the tears in regulatory frameworks and slip through them.)

3.
Urban planning has mostly been couched, perhaps unconsciously, in the notion of growing economies. Salaries and profit margins that keep up with or exceed costs of living and inflation rates, sustain a city (perhaps even demand a city) conceivable as a series of distinct zones: residential zones, commercial zones, leisure zones, tourist zones. But once economies cease to grow, this partitioned city falls apart. Laid-off workers can't continue to pay mortgages on their suburban homes or steep commuting and gas bills , businesses without profit can't stay open, empty tourist sites quickly deteriorate. The city has to be renegotiated as a collection of zones of indistinction: a house becomes a restaurant during lunch hours every day; a former shop owner now fixes cars in his garage; the backyard of the local supermarket's part-time butcher becomes a small ham-curing establishment (he pilfers pork legs at the end of his shift). It's a city of blurred edges.

1. Branzi, A 2006, Weak and Diffuse Modernity: The World of Projects at the Beginning of the 21st Century, Skira, Milan, 30.

2. de Certeau, M 1996, La Invención de lo Cotidiano: 1 Artes de Hacer, Translated by Alejandro Pescador, Universidad Iberoamericana, México.

All images by:
Gean Moreno and Ernesto Oroza

4.
As the examples just mentioned suggest, the city, facing the condition of a ghost town, already has a series of logics that may help keep the tumbleweeds from rolling in. These tactical logics are, of course, what urbanists often dismiss and discredit. They are the work of immigrants applying rudimentary knowledge from their backward countries to the 'advanced' cities of the West; they are the poor or those on the way to poverty, merely appealing to a basic survival instinct, fighting the inevitable, tooth-and-nail. What goes unsaid is that these are efforts to respond to immediate needs and draw on ground level and proven intelligences. Survival is an unmatched catalyst in the generation of real and innovative solutions. It fires up an intense astuteness in those for whom all guarantees have been taken off the table. It demands a rigorous honing of one's resourcefulness. It calls for a radical pragmatism that overturns all banal value systems that one adheres to.

5.
What we have in certain cities (or parts of them) is a race against the plywood sheets. Placed over doors and windows, they have become an easy sign to read: the home dwellers have been evicted. As they speak of the tragedy of what has occurred, these plywood sheets threaten the neighbours. The possibility that they will multiply through the area, be nailed to all the houses in the vicinity, becomes a haunting prospect. The plywood sheets may be announcing a condition that is contagious. One imagines less a slimy body that gangrene and other infections are turning to mush, than a bleached-out piece of flesh, its epidermal pigments all gone, its distinctive features erased. A body blanched by an endless spread of plywood sheets. The knots and woodgrains will become the pattern on the decorative wallpaper of a disaster that no one figured out how to avoid.

6.
In the fluid space that tactics and radical pragmatism generate, and in which they nest themselves, meanings are unstable. Objects unfurl differently at different registers and live parallel existences. The menacing plywood sheets, feared by those who have managed to keep their houses, become the walls of a kind of memory box when real estate agency signs begin to appear, hanging from their gallows-like wooden structures. If the plywood 'erases' the apertures of the house turning the structure into an impenetrable cube that casts a long shadow over the history of the family that has been sent away, the photograph of the smiling real estate agent, plasticised and contiguous with the bold logo of his/her company, is looking to erase more than just certain architectural elements. It wants to white-out the difficulties that the plywood memorialises. A virtual layer of plastic smiles intend to mantle entire neighbourhoods with the shameless promise of a sunnier future.

7.
One of these tactical logics that the city already possesses is what we call the Moire House. It's the house in which two or more functional fields meet. A single-family house, which is, for instance, both residence and ham-curing establishment, is a Moire House. It's not so much the house with the traditional office in it, a small room dedicated to business that doesn't impinge on the rest of the functions in the house, and which technological advances (desktop PCs, printers) have compacted and made discreet. It is, rather, the house in which at times it becomes unclear that its main function is residential, in which the tense exchange between incompatible demands becomes its most telling quality, its dominant marker of identity. Imagine diagramming the residential functions of a house as a pattern. Now, imagine overlaying on that a second pattern of functions not usually associated with the home: ham-curing establishment, restaurant, beauty salon, cake shop, scrap collection yard or marijuana growing house. The field of these superimposed functions, of these two patterns, would produce a Moire. In this sense, a restaurant in Little Haiti that is only open during lunch hours and sits in the middle of a living room in a house in which people still live, in which the parents have their own room and the children have their own room and the kitchen is used to cook their dinners just as much as it is used to cook lunch for dozens of customers during the day, this is a Moire House.

8.
The Moire House is suggested by strangely misplaced artefacts: a large soup cauldron in a kitchen made to serve a small family; a wrought iron gated door to a bathroom (in which, the cashier

sits during business hours); a couple of spare bedrooms fitted with agricultural equipment (hydroponic lamps, thermometers to determine humidity levels, fertiliser dispenser). It is when artefacts that respond to exigencies not usually associated to the home are found in the middle of it, that one can start to recognise or imagine the Moire House.

9.
The Moire House spreads. Its effects and demands radiate. The patterns of use that crisscross inside the house project their claims out onto the surrounding environment. The city's infrastructures and services, electricity, trash pickup, roadways and sidewalks are measurably affected. Power usage increases, the demand for parking exceeds the suburban street's capacity, a growing circulation of bodies and automobiles alter the block's level of noise, these are the rings of the radiating effects of the Moire House.

10.
An aerial view of the neighbourhood may reveal certain hyperactivity, not only in the circulation of vehicles and bodies, but also in the accumulation of materials. That is, the archetypal bird's-eye view of the suburb, with gardens and patios, white outdoor furniture, pools and the feeling of settled and unchanging space (like the image of multiplied fragments that a kaleidoscope produces) are now, suddenly, interrupted. Holes begin to appear in the pattern. They multiply and grow. One pattern eventually dissolves into another, this second one structured by proliferating absences. In the narrow side yard of a house, metal scraps picked up throughout the city uncharacteristically begin to accumulate. The part-time butcher, aside from curing ham in the evening, also collects metal on his day off to supplement his income. He'll deliver the scraps to the junkyard when there's enough of it to make the trip worth it. It may take a while. In a nearby neighbourhood, a drywaller, usually one of the last people called into the construction site, brings home leftover cinder blocks and stacks them by the A/C. Eventually, he'll sell them. In the meantime, however, the piles of junk/construction materials/potential money grow into alien protuberances on lawns intended for careful manicuring. Weeds grow out of them. They interrupt the suburb's uniform layout. Holes in the pattern.

11.
Another home owner, on the other side of town, runs a makeshift salon in her living room. It'll stay open until the neighbour can no longer tolerate the increased volume of cars as they overflow onto her driveway, bog down her lawn, seep into another neighbour's lawn and eventually spill down the street and wrap around the block. The situation is aggravated by a second business: she bakes cakes. A complex system of display cases structures her family room. There's a pair of love seats between all the vitrines for the clients, and a vast library of photo albums neatly shelved. In the albums are images of all her previous productions, a range that seduces the client into believing that he or she can stretch their imagination as a far as they want, and all for a reasonable price. This house, if we momentarily ignore its residential usage, is a Venn Diagram of two functional business patterns: the two circles meet in the kitchen, when a cake is baking in the oven and the depilatory wax is boiling on the stove. It's an intensely olfactory intersection.

12.
Behaviours are altered by the Moire House. Work schedules change. They may no longer happen in blocks: nine to five is replaced by a different set of hours or by many sets of hours. One's schedule can become that of the night-cleaning crews and the graveyard-shift toll collectors, but it can just as easily break up into small spans of time between breakfast and the Jerry Springer show, between Springer and picking up the kids from school, between the end of school and football practice, between football practice and the late news. Domestic rhythms begin to determine production schedules and operating hours. And, in fact, things may be even harder than that to pin down. Stealing the pork leg in the morning for an evening of curing is like a stretched appendage of the work schedule, a quick and necessary action.

13.
Children are an important part of the Moire House. They are a force that unwittingly demands all sorts of alterations and additions. They prevent the home from becoming just a business. There is a seemingly ethical imperative to maintain a semblance of a home for their sake. Side doors are installed for clients so that the front door remains an entrance to a home. In fact, all kinds of new paths are carved out and elements added. Rows of pavers lead from the driveway, along the side of the house, to the 'client's door.' Small, unimpressive bathrooms are built for clientele, 'public' bathrooms, compared to the private ones that only the family can use.

14.
If the pattern of functions of the beauty salon, the curing establishment and the junk metal collector 'enlarge' the house, the actual residential patterns of the single-family home decrease as foreclosures and unemployment empty houses at a steady clip. Two extreme forces, each tugging in a different direction, radically change the shape of the suburb. Emptiness, viewed from above, extends like a stain, spooks the neighbourhood. It can be contained solely by a radical and unsentimental pragmatism; paradoxically, only the repurposing of domestic space into productive space and serviceable areas can maintain the family atmosphere of the suburb. That is, only by altering this atmosphere can the Moire House save it. This is its unshakeable alibi, what allows it to reveal itself as a necessary typology for an emptying city.

15.
Even after new uses settle into the domestic space and the home businesses begin to prosper, their physiognomy can only be proposed or understood laterally, through alterations in the diagrams of internal and external circulation. One finds clues in analyses of energy consumption and comparative studies of phone, electricity, gas and water bills, in statistics concerned with noise and air pollution levels. There are also the informal surveys that provide a record of less quantifiable things, such as the concern of parents over children playing in the increasingly travelled street. In other words, as the domestic signs of the facades and the general exterior physiognomy of the suburban house remain nearly unaltered, invisible structures, fleshed out in the changing density of flows, in new expenses, in altered schedules and agendas, propose, in conjunction with certain alterations inside the house, a new typology that, while transitory, is as efficient as any model optimised for urban experience. The utility bills are the blueprints of these invisible structures we are calling Moire Houses.

Jason Ho

:

LIVING ON THE LINE: A SEARCH FOR SHARED LANDSCAPES

There is no denying boundary walls exist in China and have bearings on the socio-economic, psychological and corporeal spaces of those who live within the walls and those who are outside them. Indeed, most urban design literature regards boundary walls negatively and would support their eradication. Living on the Line recognises the impacts of boundary walls, but it still aims to provide an inkling of how lives are lived positively, despite these walls. It shows how, over time, people have used boundary walls as physical and social structures to help move beyond the bounds and territories imposed on them. To do this, the project maps the lived experiences of a number of vendors whose businesses operate around a boundary wall encircling Jimei University in Xiamen, China, to understand how a boundary wall can be 'broken' or transgressed to allow a 'shared landscape' to emerge. Mapping the vendors leads to a consideration of boundary from a wider perspective and an understanding of the territories and boundaries as a network of relationships.

Gated communities are becoming the dominant form of community lifestyle in contemporary Chinese cities. Walls and fences are omnipresent around university campuses, apartment complexes, urban parks, tourist resorts, office parks and industrial parks. The ceaseless construction of boundary walls across suburbs and cities destroys street life and privatises urban resources, thus causing social, cultural and economic segregation and marginalisation of certain socio-economic groups. The gap between the wealthy and the extremely poor is exacerbated by the decreasing opportunities for peoples of different social groups to interact and this can lead to conflicts and tensions.

Looking at the boundary wall that circumnavigates Jimei University's grounds, one might easily surmise that the wall represents China's move towards increasing privatisation. Surveillance cameras and at least five security kiosks, staffed by armed guards, are located at various points along the wall where the campus and the village meet. Students need to present their personal IDs to the gatekeepers on duty to enter the campus. Within the university, students also require electronic security pass-cards to move from their dormitories (the 'Living Zone') to the lecture halls and the library, and to the indoor sports centre and leisure facilities (the 'Activity Zone'). These differentiated levels of access stratify

Above. A farmer in Xiamen's Jimei District viewing his razed house and orchards that will eventually become a new campus for the Jimei Fisheries College.

Right. Xiamen is a major city on the southeast (Taiwan Strait) coast of China. It is one of the four original Special Economic Zones opened to foreign investment and trade when China began economic reforms in the early 1980s. It is at the frontline of China's new urbanization and where massive urban transformations are currently taking place. Today, various types of gated communities are dominating Xiamen's cityscape, turning it into a city of walls.

the campus and even the village around it into hierarchical zones. On the lowest rung are the villagers, perceived as rural and uneducated, who cannot enter the university unless to perform menial duties.

When the villagers lost their farmland due to the new university, they lost their jobs and sources of income. Although the university's boundary wall prevents them from entering the campus to seek alternative jobs/income, the villagers have found opportunities for micro-economies to occur at the wall. Instead of being a political public-private division, the wall acts more like an urban 'magnet', drawing acts of social, economic and cultural exchange and interaction, symbolising a joint between two distinct communities. These acts are in situ, ad hoc, responsive and specific, working to blur the territorial demarcation and create a space that moves beyond the binary of private-university versus public-village lane. What is produced through these exchanges is a picture of a wider area - beyond the immediate vicinity of the boundary wall - where an interrelated web of acts of informal activity or transgression occur. Yet, transgressions or informal activities are never isolated acts; they are always part of a wider system. One might suggest that, beneath the formal rational divisions seen in Chinese cities, there lies an informal landscape of conversations and dialogues that escape dominant socio-economic discourse.

The boundary wall, which keeps students and villagers away from each other, now becomes a physical apparatus used to set up makeshift shops and hide from the law if necessary. While the separation of the campus and the village still physically remains, one might nonetheless suggest the boundary wall, which was once the 'centrepiece' of campus security, is now just one of the pieces in a game of unofficial economic exchanges. The boundary wall as divider still physically divides but it is simultaneously a tool and a site for many socio-economic groups to converge and create communities which are both temporary and mercantile. However, that its function swings from a divider to something that offers refuge from patrolling policemen - and, more importantly, is a site of transaction - is owed to the very specific conditions of the boundary.

Many villagers in Xiamen's Jimei District continue to grow vegetables on construction sites (their former farmland) before the construction projects begin.

Opposite:
A row of ladders leaning against the university's boundary wall.

In 2012, according to statistics from Jimei University, there were at least 500 vendors operating unregistered businesses along the university's boundaries.

Delivery between Sun Cuo Village's vendors and Jimei University students at lunch hour time.

Kees Lokman

WICKED PROBLEMS ALONG CANADA'S CARBON CORRIDOR

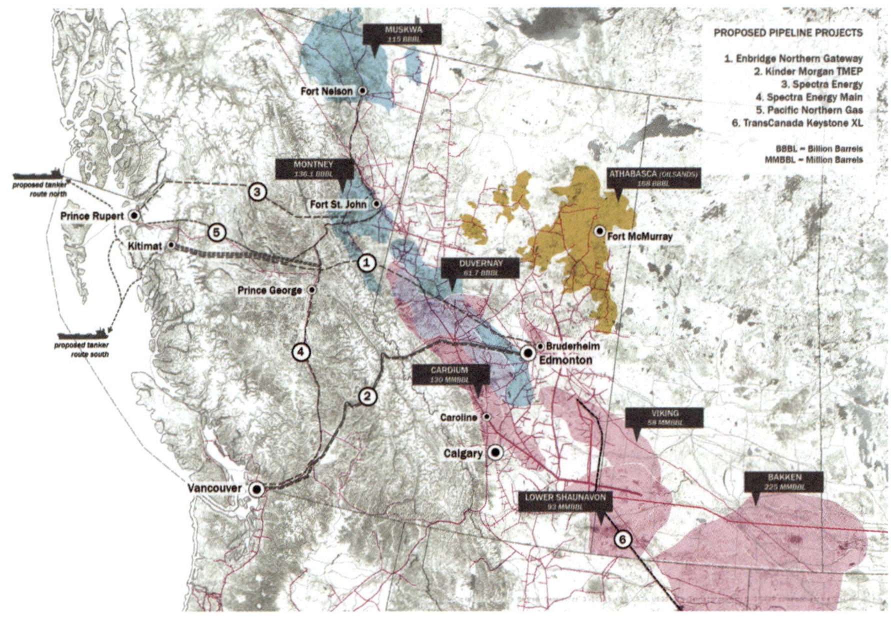

Canada's carbon corridor.

In recent decades, as a result of the growing economies in Asia and South America, the demand for energy has increased substantially. The International Energy Agency, the world's leading multilateral energy organisation, has estimated that by 2040 global energy demands will increase by 30 per cent.[1] This is already producing wholly new 'energy geographies'.[2] On the one hand, there is a rapid growth in the implementation of renewable energy projects, including wind farms, solar fields and hydroelectric dams. On the other, we can see a significant increase in the extraction of unconventional fossil fuels such as shale gas (through hydraulic fracking) and oil-sands mining. This is nowhere more pertinent than in Canada's carbon corridor – an interconnected web of major oil, gas, coal and hydroelectric projects across British Columbia and Alberta. The corridor is home to the largest shale gas deposits in North America as well as the third-largest proven crude oil reserve in the world. Accelerated exploitation of these resources is driving large-scale infrastructural developments, environmental transformations, demographic shifts and geopolitical conflict. For those involved in the analysis and design of landscapes, this raises a number of important questions, including: what new landscapes are emerging as a result of the extraction, processing and distribution of energy resources? How do these landscapes function socially, spatially and ecologically? And, how can designers play a role in helping to examine, communicate and provide potential solutions to address the cumulative and cross-scale impacts of resource extraction?

Wicked problems

Mining, energy and mineral exploration have always been key economic drivers for both British Columbia and Alberta, contributing to jobs, investments and innovation in engineering, technology and the construction industry. However, the speed, magnitude and geographic extent of ongoing developments are increasingly creating conflicts. Recently implemented or proposed resource developments within the carbon corridor

1. The International Energy Agency 2016, 'World Energy Outlook: Executive Summary', The International Energy Agency, <https://www.iea.org/publications/freepublications/publication/WorldEnergyOutlook2016ExecutiveSummaryEnglish.pdf>.

2. Calvert, K 2015, Progress in Human Geography, DOI: 10.1177/0309132514566343.

3. Booth, AL & Skelton, NW 2011, 'Industry and government perspectives on first nations' participation in the British Columbia environmental assessment process', Environmental Impact Assessment Review, vol. 31, no. 3, pp. 216–25.

4. Everingham, JA, Collins, N, Cavaye, J, Rifkin, W, Vink, S, Baumgartl, T & Rodriguez, D 2016, 'Energy from the foodbowl: associated land-use conflicts, risks and wicked problems', Landscape and Urban Planning, no. 154, pp. 68–80.

include: two large-scale hydroelectric dams, eleven mines, eight wind farms, over 10,000 oil and gas well sites, and six new pipelines (for gas and bitumen transportation).[3] Beyond drastically altering the physical form and functioning of landscapes, energy resource extraction also contributes to a diminished sense of place and fractures local communities. As a result, the carbon corridor has become a locus of social, political and environmental conflicts as extraction industries, farmers, First Nations communities, conservation groups and municipalities have sharp differences of opinion on how to best utilise the natural resources in this fairly remote part of Canada.

Design theorists Horst Rittel and Melvin M Webber introduced the term 'wicked problem' to describe these kinds of complex challenges that involve multiple stakeholders with differing values and perspectives. Incomplete knowledge, uncertainty and divergent interests make it difficult for subject-matter experts, planners and policy makers to provide solutions that work for all parties involved. Everingham et al. claim that 'Because of the complex, multi-disciplinary nature of cumulative impacts - whether social, environmental, or economic - issues are often oversimplified, misrepresented, or represented in a fragmented way'.[4] In order to provide possible solutions to these wicked problems, we need new methods to adequately portray and communicate the interconnectedness and cumulative effects of human activities and different land uses over both space and time.

Energy geographies

Until recently, research and scholarship examining the human-environment-energy nexus have primarily come from the fields of geography, forestry, political ecology and anthropology. That the topic is largely overlooked from a spatial design perspective is a significant shortcoming. Designers and, in particular, landscape architects have reached a certain maturity in examining the interrelations of the formal, symbolic and pictorial representations of landscapes on the one hand, and the formal and material consequences of spatial processes and practices on the other. Their unique cultural perception, combined with the emergence of new conceptual frameworks, analytical tools and design approaches, positions designers well to contribute significantly to the debate about the future of energy geographies.

Correspondingly, energy production, distribution and consumption reinforces climate change and ongoing urbanisation, threatens food and water security, and is therefore a matter of social justice. As such, the notion of energy geographies as both conceptual framework and spatial condition should be at the forefront of contemporary design discourse. Stremke and van den Dobbelsteen have argued that 'the sheer quantity of ... energy that needs to be generated to sustain humanity may require us to regard, at least conceptually, every landscape as an energy landscape'.[5] This 'reordering of our priorities through that of energy', Van der Horst and Nadaï imply, 'is bringing a new angle to the questions "what makes landscapes?" And "what are landscapes made for?". It is an occasion to revisit the relevance of the ways and tools we have at hand to approach landscapes.'[6]

The agency of mapping

Perhaps the most important contribution that designers can make in order to advance discussions on energy geographies is through mapping, diagramming and visual narratives. This representational approach has the ability to portray interconnections between energy sources and energy sinks, as well as other seen and unseen aspects of energy geographies, such as waste, infrastructures, political boundaries, wildlife migration corridors and social imaginaries.[7] As pointed out by James Corner in his seminal essay 'The Agency of Mapping': 'Through rendering visible multiple and sometimes disparate field conditions, mapping allows for an understanding of terrain as only the surface expression of a complex and dynamic imbroglio of social and natural processes.'[8] The creative process of representation allows designers to uncover and reformulate physical and symbolic layers of the built environment. It is through this continual process of investigation, discovery and remapping that landscapes derive meaning and new knowledge of the built environment is produced.

5. Stremke, S & van den Dobbelsteen, A 2013, Sustainable energy landscapes: designing, planning, and development, CRC Press, Boca Raton, FL.

6. van der Horst, D & Nadaï, A 2010, 'Introduction: landscapes of energies', Landscape Research, vol. 35, no. 2, pp. 143–155.

7. Ghosn, R & Jazairy, EH 2017, 'Geography and oil: the territory of externalities', in Infrastructure Space, I & A Ruby (eds), Ruby Press, Berlin, pp. 361–376.

8. Corner, J 1999, 'The agency of mapping: speculation, critique and invention', in Mappings, D Cosgrove (ed.), Reaktion Books, London, pp. 214–252.

9. Neuman, M 2006, 'Infiltrating infrastructures: on the nature of networked infrastructure', Journal of Urban Technology, vol. 13, no. 1, pp. 3–31.

10. Mitchell, WJ 2003, Me++: The Cyborg Self and the Networked City, MIT Press, Cambridge, MA.

11. Anderson, M 2010, '$1.7 billion and rising: taxpayers' gas bill for oil sands', The Tyee Online, <https://thetyee.ca/News/2010/11/09/GasBillForOilSands/>.

12. Green, SJ, Demes, K, Arbeider, M, Palen, WJ, Salomon, AK, Sisk, TD, Webster, M & Ryan ME 2017, 'Oil sands and the marine environment: current knowledge and future challenges', Frontiers in Ecology and the Environment, vol. 15, no. 2, pp. 74–83.

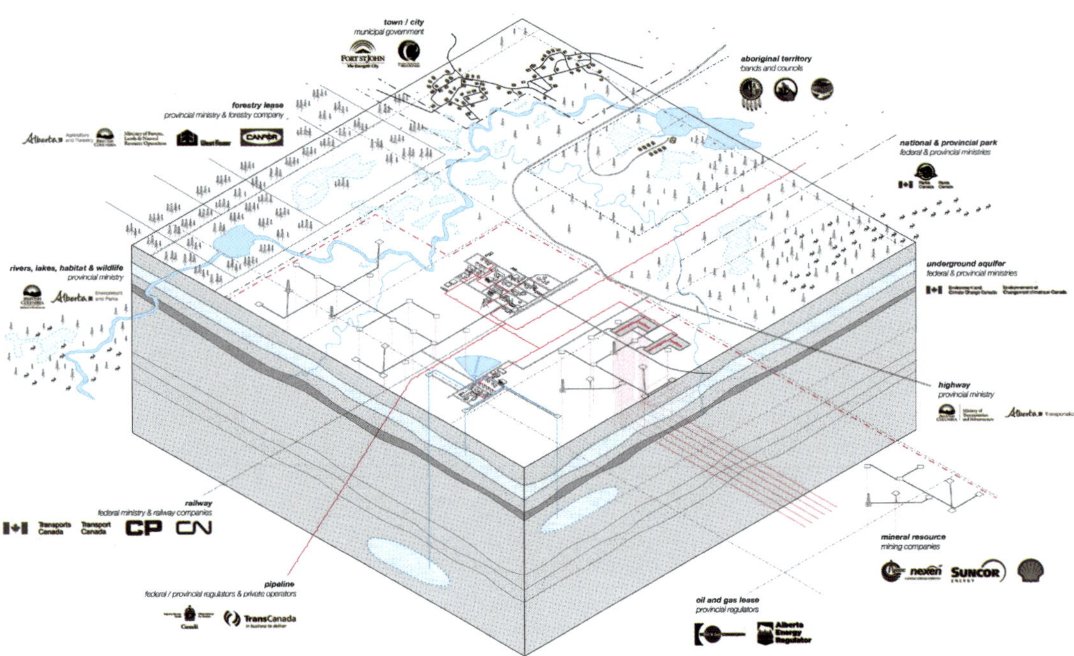

Energy geographies: actors, space claims.

Opposite:
Oil sands: resource flows.

Infrastructure networks are particularly important in both the understanding and representation of energy geographies. As interfaces between human-made and natural systems, networked infrastructures can be understood as life supports fully embedded in our environments.[9] They actively reshape social, ecological, political and physical relationships by rearranging the flows of water, waste and soil. Urban theorist William J Mitchell beautifully captures the complex material and socio-spatial entanglements created by networked infrastructures:

> Water supply and sewer networks have become geographic extensions of my alimentary canal, my respiratory system, and associated organic plumbing. The carbon-based systems that circulate solids, fluids, and gases within my bag of skin are connected to a vast, external, mostly metallic and plastic network of pipes, ducts, pumps, processing plants, and mechanical transportation devices for food, water, conditioned air, and waste disposal. These extended networks collect resources in distant and dispersed catchment zones, concentrate them at storage nodes, transfer them to consumption nodes, and eventually disperse waste to disposal zones.[10]

With this in mind, we can imagine creating visual representations showing the material transformations and geographic extents of bitumen production from remote areas, transported and distributed through an interconnected network of infrastructures, to distant urban areas to power household appliances. At the same time, these metabolic processes can be drawn in relation to the socio-spatial and political implications of energy developments, such as the displacement of both people and non-humans, as well as geopolitical conflict among provinces and nations.

Visual narratives

This ongoing research aims to chart these issues by testing and developing a range of different representational techniques. Focusing on the agency of mapping, I will highlight three of many possible storylines to reflect some of the divergent implications of energy extraction along Canada's carbon corridor.

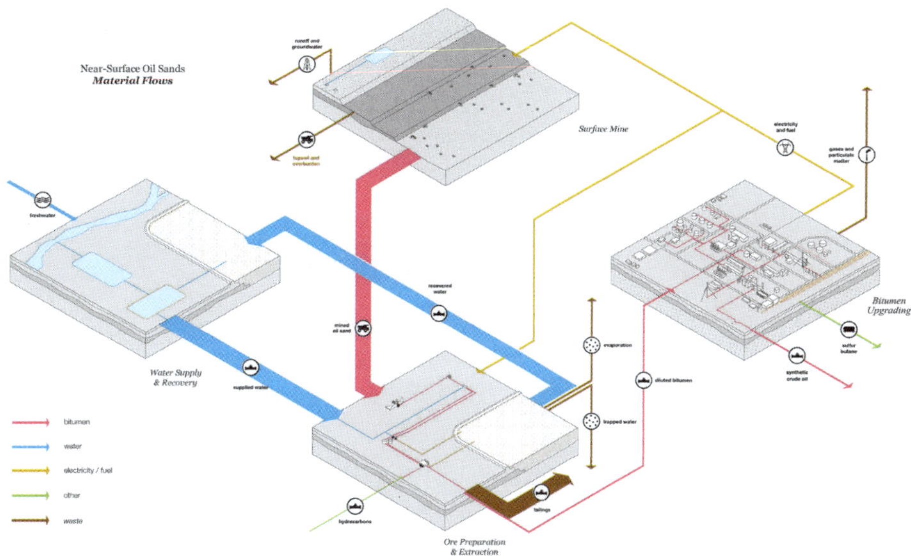

These visual narratives investigate notions of 1) uneven development and externalities (spatial and temporal inertia), 2) the boom-bust cycle (temporary labour and real estate speculation), and 3) displacement and fragmentation (of habitats and social structures). They seek to provide a provisional understanding of the region by offering a textured and multidimensional picture of several separate, yet interconnected, issues associated with resource extraction activities.

1. Uneven developments and externalities

Energy developments in the carbon corridor have widespread implications that affect landscapes and livelihoods from the hyperlocal to the global. Increased demands for natural gas in Japan, for example, fuel new investments in oil-sands mining for hydraulic fracking in British Columbia and Alberta. This, in turn, spurs proposals for new pipelines, processing plants and ports. Fracking developments require substantial amounts of water (drawn from rivers, lakes and local aquifers), high-quality frac sand (imported from Wisconsin), land for storage of wastewater and stockpiling of displaced topsoil, as well as massive inputs of energy (partially paid for by taxpayers).[11] The location, supply and disposal of these resources are distributed unevenly, which means certain landscapes, species, communities and people are impacted more than others. Although oil-sands mining happens over 1000 kilometres away from coastlines, it negatively impacts marine environments and coastal ecosystems by increasing shipping volumes, bitumen/chemical spills and noise pollution. At the same time, oil sands contribute significantly to greenhouse gas emission, which leads to ocean acidification, temperature increase and sea level rise.[12]

2. The boom-bust cycle

Due to highly volatile oil prices, the intensity and magnitude of oil-sands operations have fluctuated significantly over the past decade. To compensate for this, the industry relies primarily on temporary labour, with the former industrial regions of Atlantic Canada being the most important sources of the mobile workforce. 'The relationship is symbiotic: Communities in Eastern Canada supply labourers for the resource-rich West, while western paycheques build new homes and buy new trucks in the Maritimes'.[13] In concert with the inflows and outflows of temporary migrant labourers, Calgary's commercial real estate market rises and falls with the volatile market. With the plummeting oil prices of late, multinational corporations have downsized and laid off thousands of workers. As a result, many recently completed office towers not only remain vacant, their values have diminished by nearly $4 billion CAD.[14] These speculations also leave their marks on the territory. Alberta and British Columbia are dotted with thousands of suspended and abandoned wells, which pose a variety of social, environmental and financial risks. Most inactive well sites leak methane and contaminate soils

13. Freeman, S 2014, 'The 4000km Commute', Huffpost, <http://www.huffingtonpost.ca/2014/12/16/miramichi-oilsands-alberta-working-poor_n_6335842.html>.

14. Cryderman, K & McMahon, T 2017, 'Oil slump hammers Calgary's downtown office real estate market', Globe and Mail, <https://www.theglobeandmail.com/real-estate/calgary-and-edmonton/oil-slump-hammers-calgarys-downtown-office-real-estate-market/article33520672/>.

15. Pearson, TW 2016, 'Frac sand mining and the disruption of place, landscape, and community in Wisconsin', Human Organization, Spring 2016, vol. 75, no. 1, p. 47.

16. Bishop, ID 2015, 'Location based information to support understanding of landscape futures', Landscape and Urban Planning no. 142, pp. 120-31.

17. UBC School of Architecture and Landscape Architecture 2017, 'Landscapes of Energy', <https://sala.ubc.ca/news-events/feature-stories/2017-04-19-landscapes-energy>.

18. Ghosn, R & Jazairy, EH 2017, 'Geography and oil: the territory of externalities', in Infrastructure Space, I & A Ruby (eds), Ruby Press, Berlin, pp. 361-376.

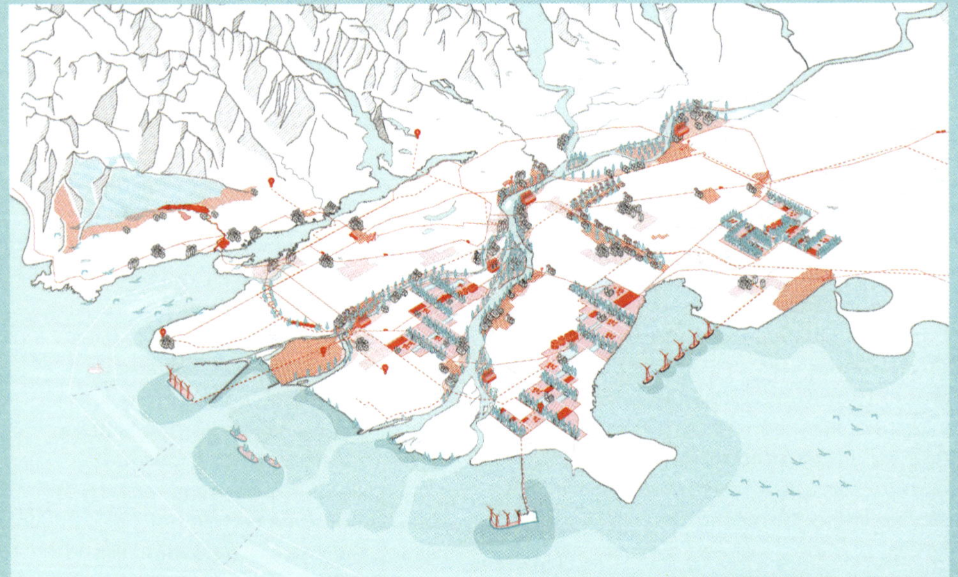

Above:
Fraser river.

Bottom:
Regional strategy.

Opposite:
In-situ oil sands: landscape transformations.

In-Situ Oil Sands
Landscape Transformation

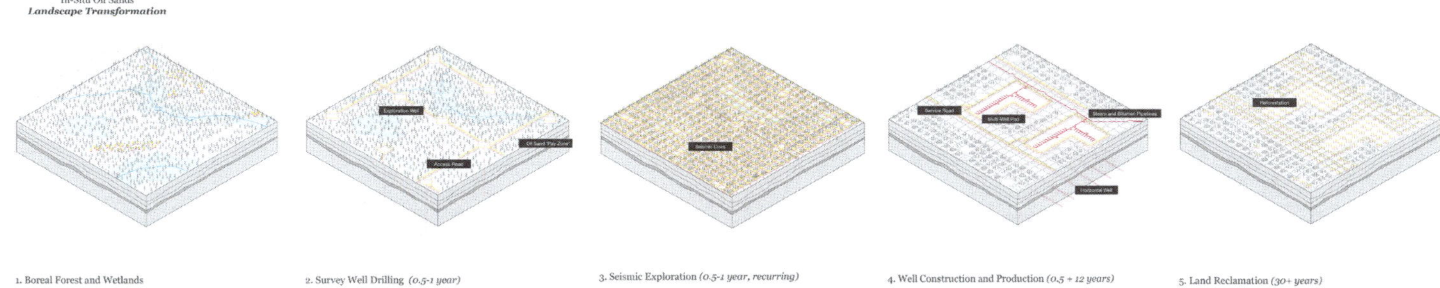

1. Boreal Forest and Wetlands 2. Survey Well Drilling *(0.5-1 year)* 3. Seismic Exploration *(0.5-1 year, recurring)* 4. Well Construction and Production *(0.5 + 12 years)* 5. Land Reclamation *(30+ years)*

and groundwater while their presence devalues property and prevents farmers making full use of their land.

3. Displacement and fragmentation

Energy developments along the carbon corridor are managed by a complex regulatory and legal framework involving dozens of different intentions and cultural perceptions of the landscape. While provinces are legally obligated to consult and accommodate First Nations on any land and resource decisions that could impact their livelihoods, they usually do not make the approach until the very late stages of planning processes. As a result, First Nations are often unsuccessful in stopping energy companies from exploitation of their lands. As Pearson writes, 'In a potent symbol of "creative destruction", the remnants of previous ways of life are destroyed to make way for a new extractive industry generating billions of dollars in profit for out-of-state investors'.[15] Alongside the displacement and fragmentation of people and communities, non-humans are also significantly impacted by the large-scale transformation of the landscape. The magnitude of seismic lines, for example, have completely changed the predator–prey relationship between wolves and caribou, leading to a drastic decline in caribou populations. With the substantial inertia that exists in ecological systems, it is difficult to predict the impacts of energy developments, as well as the effectiveness of remediation efforts. This is particularly so because time lags may occur between a change in a driver and the time when the full consequences of that change become apparent.

By increasing our ability to portray the complex socio-ecological relations of energy geographies across a range of spatial and temporal scales, these mappings and visualisations have the ability to alter the ways in which people perceive the environments. As argued by Bishop, 'changes in the environment are critical, but changes in the viewer can have a profound influence on attitudes to environmental change'.[16] Appropriately situated, the possibilities enabled by mapping can assist in the transmission of critical spatial knowledge and ideas about landscapes among interdisciplinary groups and with diverse stakeholders. This, in turn, can positively influence changes in social and cultural practices, and strengthen energy planning and policies in a number of settings.

Energy futures and design speculation

In addition to rendering visible the socio-spatial conditions and uneven geographic developments of energy systems, designers can also speculate on and explore the possibilities of shaping more just and resilient relationships between economy and ecology. I recently taught a research seminar entitled 'Landscapes of Energy' at the University of British Columbia, which explored these concepts. After students examined the challenges, opportunities and socio-spatial implications of various renewable energy sources (wind, solar, hydro, biofuels and waste-to-energy) they were challenged to look at ways in which energy generation could be incorporated into the Metro Vancouver Region.[17] With a focus on co-benefits and minimisation of externalities, students worked in pairs to identify locations within the urban fabric where energy generation could be coupled with food production, habitat creation, ecological revitalisation, climate change adaptation and urban development. Shifting between the local and regional scale, these drawings articulate the designer's tools and agency in articulating how existing projects, waste flows, infrastructures and social-ecological systems can be re-imagined. Lower Mainland dairy farming operations can produce biogas to cut down greenhouse gas emissions, and provide additional income by selling excess electricity to the grid. Restoration of riparian corridors and forest ecosystems can be coupled with short-and long-rotation forestry to provide energy crops. And ongoing dredging operations and plans for the expansion of Deltaport provide opportunities to create a series of barrier islands in order to protect the coastline from storm surges, create marine habitat and integrate offshore wind energy.

Conclusion

The Anthropocene is driven by a fossil fuel-based global energy supply system. Energy developments associated with this system exploit space. Its operations, infrastructures and byproducts impact people, ecosystems and power relations across a range of scales. Although renewable energy is making great advances, these energy sources, too, create their own social, spatial, environmental and political frictions. By synthesising and drawing relationships, design has the agency to integrate multidisciplinary perspectives. Here, the challenge is not simply to visualise and represent these systems, but to intervene in them in ways that address the socio-spatial contradictions and conflicts inherent in the production of energy landscapes. As pointedly remarked by Rania Ghosn, designers have to understand the political and ethical implications of their work 'all the while imagining fantastic survival and adaptation strategies that invite us to make sense of the world and re-envision it in ways that generate inquisitive, delightful, and potentially subversive responses'.[18]

Lizzie Yarina

:

PORIRUA PASIFIKA: A PACIFIC UTOPIA IN AOTEAROA

The settlers of the Pacific were mobile canoe navigators who saw the ocean not as a medium of isolation, but rather as a fluid connector of distant isles.[1] The first migrants to Aotearoa (New Zealand) were Polynesian navigators, who voyaged to the 'land of the long white cloud' more than 800 years ago. Even after settling Aotearoa, Māori continued to navigate thousands of miles to the Cook and Society Islands.[2]

The invisible lines of national territory that colonists drew across maps of the ocean paralysed the oceanic mobility of Polynesians and other Pacific Islanders, interrupting an ongoing dialogue between Māori and their Pasifika cousins. The hard lines associated with private property and the contemporary nation-state, trap atoll dwellers (inhabitants of low-lying coral islands) in 'sinking' nations. Meanwhile, the same states that colonised and divided the Pacific are the primary culprits for greenhouse gases causing the seas to rise.

Porirua Pasifika proposes a utopian future for a decolonised Aotearoa that celebrates the spatial values of local *iwi* (Māori tribes), while seeking to unravel the subdivision of the Pacific, returning free movement to oceanic migrants. In particular, Porirua, already the de-facto capital of Tokelau and a major Pacific-Islander city, becomes a hub of culturally-adapted space for those atoll dwellers whose entire nations are under threat as a result of rising seas. Rather than negating Māori heritage, these spaces could be in dialogue with local Māori and their sacred sites. Already, the many Pasifika communities in Porirua are in conversation with *iwi* and one another; in 2012, Tokelau-Atafu islanders created a *vaka* (canoe) in collaboration with local *iwi*, who assisted in sourcing and blessing the wood for the boat. Similarly, the Atafu *umu*, or cooking pit pavilion, is shared with other communities, such as Tuvaluans and Cook Islanders, who lack such a site. Porirua Pasifika proposes amplifying these spaces of cross-cultural practice and exchange through a network of interventions that accommodate and celebrate Pacific Island communities.

This Pacific utopia in Aotearoa generates Pasifika space through both landscape and architectural interventions, expanding territory for cultural memory and living practices. Drawing on the central role of water (*wai/vai/mam/dan*) across Pacific cultures, the harbour is re-claimed as a space of connection. This is achieved by subverting the British imported model of the 'green belt', particularly to the southeast, where it divides the primarily Pasifika communities of Cannons Creek from the waterfront and the rest of the city.

Around the harbour, meaningful historic Māori ecosystems are restored along with new hybrid biomes, acting as green fingers, which stitch the city together around and through the water. This ecological reconfiguration, supported by a network of paths and arteries, re-establishes Māori and Pasifika inspired relationships to (urban) landscape. This remaking of a Pasifika Aotearoa also draws on Māori histories of pan-island ecological hybrids, such as the historic cultivation of the tropical mulberry tree to supply tapa cloth.[3] Supporting this network, hothouse conservatories propagate flora essential to atoll/islander identities and create spaces within (pools, *fale*, kitchens) for communities to

1. Hau'Ofa, E, Waddell, E & Naidu, V 1993, A New Oceania: Rediscovering Our Sea of Islands, The University of the South Pacific, Suva, Fiji, 2-16.

2. Somerville, A.T.P 2012, Once Were Pacific: Māori Connections to Oceania, University of Minnesota Press, Minneapolis MN & London.

3. Ibid.

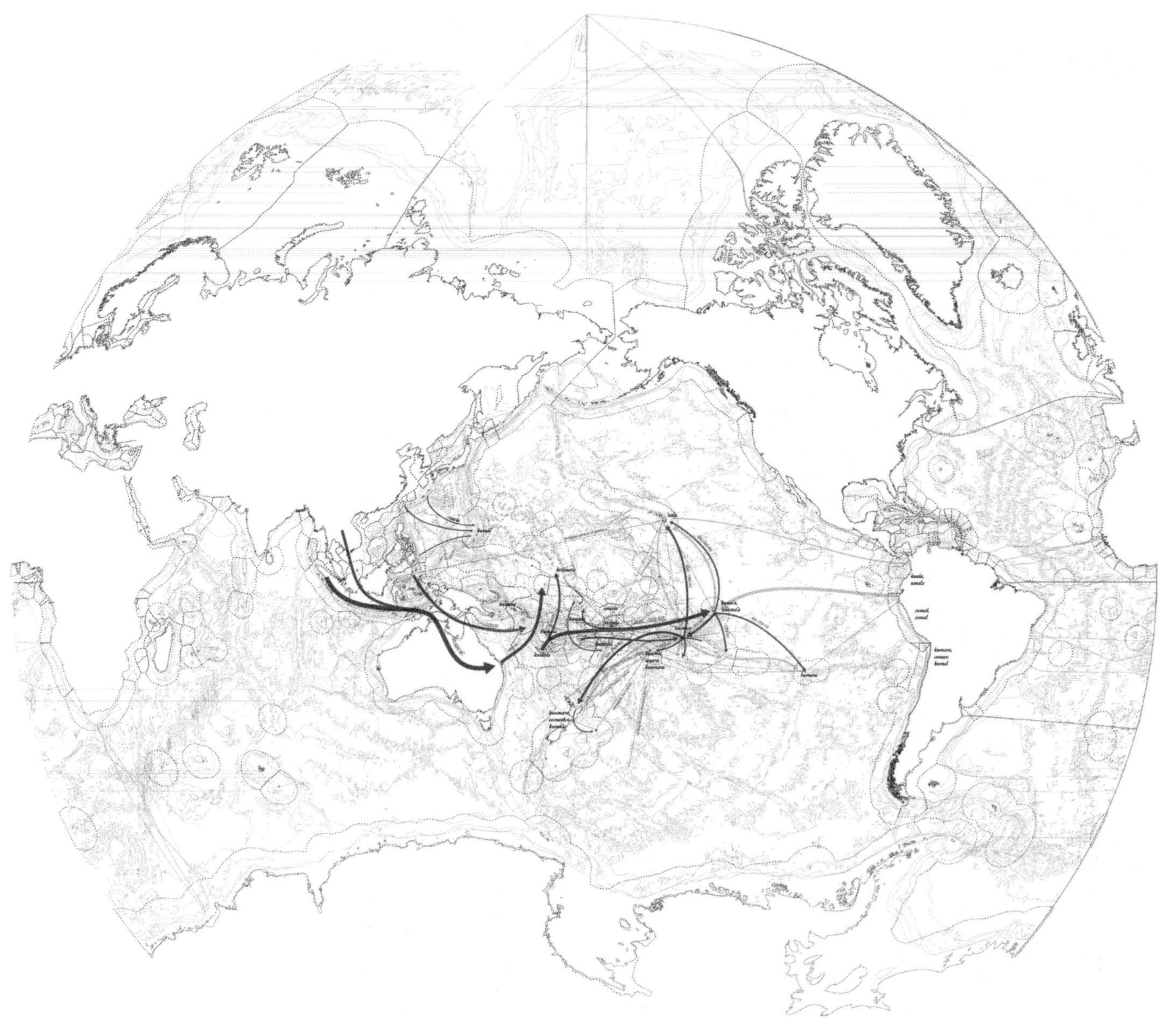

Above:
Early migration
Historically atoll-dwellers would simply find a new island when theirs became uninhabitable, but as climate change threatens their very survival, atoll denizens now find themselves paralysed by Western notions of land-tenure and nationhood.

The decolonisation of Aotearoa would mean not only interpreting city and space-making through Māori values, but also erasing colonial borders drawn across the surface of the Pacific, creating space for those island-nation-communities whose very existence is threatened by rising seas. As a possible decolonised future, this project proposes Porirua Pasifika: A Pacific Utopia in Aotearoa.

soak in the pandanus and coconut palms. These conservatories can also provide a local source for indigenous Pacific Island foods, which cannot be cultivated in subtropical climates.

A series of structures – hosted by particular island communities but shared across cultures – claim new space for cultural practices, anchored around the harbor. Collectively owned housing compounds modelled on Māori *papakainga* allow extended family networks to share space and resources, and trace along the green fingers, which reconnect the city to its harbor. A festival pavilion accommodates the many celebrations hosted by specific communities and across cultures. Interventions in the harbor accommodate diverse relationships with the sea, such as canoeing, aquatic foraging and fishing practices. Pasifika communities and collaborations already form a virtual network across Porirua, Aotearoa, the Pacific and beyond. This project explores a possible future where these systems are made visible and amplified, dissolving post-colonial spatial subdivisions and reconnecting old and new Pacific communities around the Porirua harbour. Networked across Porirua, this project explores how the city can be reclaimed not only for Māori spatial values but also as a city of the Pacific, which embraces the region's migratory identity and the diverse, interrelated cultures of Pacific Islanders.

Left:
Aotearoa is host to the world's largest Pacific city, Auckland. The population of Porirua, just outside of Wellington, is twenty-five per cent Pasifika.

Right:
Porirua is already a Pasifika city with Pacific Islander institutions and neighbourhoods superimposed onto a colonial fabric. These communities are in ongoing dialogue with local *iwi* as they seek to translate their island-based practices to Aotearoa. However, their neighbourhoods are cut off by suburban patterns and the European green belt model to the southeast.

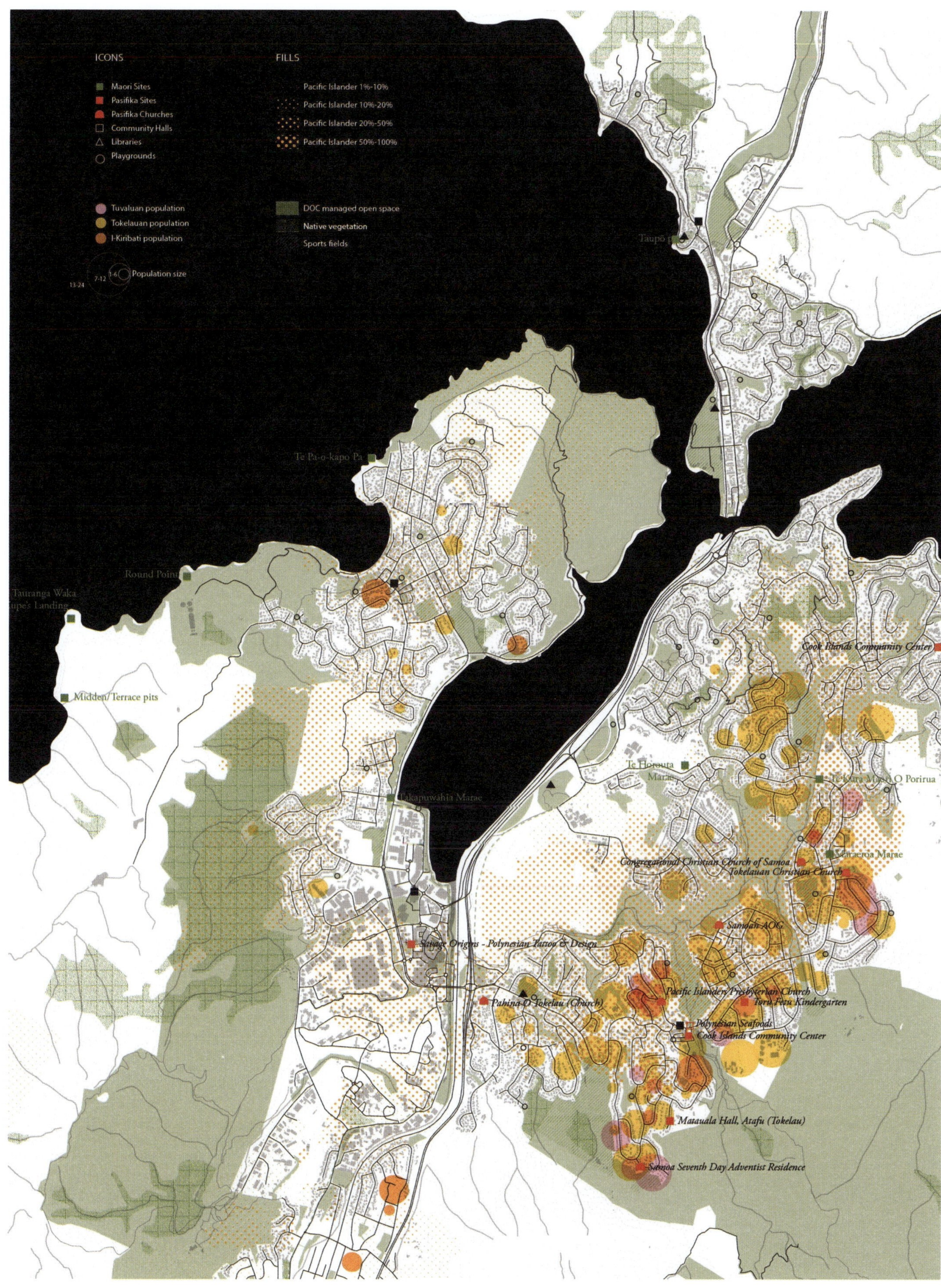
ICONS
Maori Sites
Pasifika Sites
Pasifika Churches
Community Halls
Libraries
Playgrounds
FILLS
Pacific Islander 1%-10%
Pacific Islander 10%-20%
Pacific Islander 20%-50%
Pacific Islander 50%-100%
Tuvaluan population
Tokelauan population
I-Kiribati population
DOC managed open space
Native vegetation
Sports fields
13-24
7-12
1-6
Population size
Taupo
Te Pa-o-kapo Pa
Round Point
Tauranga Waka
Midden/Terrace pits
Takapuwahia Marae
Cook Islands Community Center
Te Horouta Marae
Te Kura Maori O Porirua
Maraeroa Marae
Congregational Christian Church of Samoa
Tokelauan Christian Church
Samoan AOG
Savage Origins - Polynesian Tattoo & Design
Pacific Islanders Presbyterian Church
Toru Fetu Kindergarten
Pahina O Tokelau (Church)
Polynesian Seafoods
Cook Islands Community Center
Mataulala Hall, Atafu (Tokelau)
Samoa Seventh Day Adventist Residence

Above left:
Fishing Harbour: a fishing lagoon, with platforms and sandbars that allow for a combination of Māori, Pacific Islander, and conventional fishing methods along with aquatic foraging.

Above right:
Forest Foraging: a foraging forest, where traditional Māori foods can be collected and Polynesian permaculture can be cultivated.

Left:
Workshop: a space for traditional and traditional-hybrid craft production, such as weaving and carving. Cultural knowledge combined with new tools can create new art forms and methodologies, allowing traditional crafts to evolve.

Above:
Vakawaka House:
a cross-cultural boathouse that houses the specific traditional technologies of different islands and communities under a shared roof.

Below:
Collective House:
a system for cooperatively-owned collective housing as an alternative to the Western suburb, which accommodates extended families and kinship networks. The housing can draw on Polynesian or Micronesian architectural typologies, which disperse functions across a shared compound.

GANGSTERCOMPUTERGODWORLDWIDE
SECRET CONTAINMENT POLICY
WWW

C O N T E S T E D
C O N T E S T E D
C O N T E S T E D
C O N T E S T E D
C O N T E S T E D
C O N T E S T E D
C O N T E S T E D
D I S R U P T I V E
D I S R U P T I V E
D I S R U P T I V E
D I S R U P T I V E
D I S R U P T I V E

Alexandra Mei

:

RISE: A GUIDE TO BOUNDARY RESISTANCE

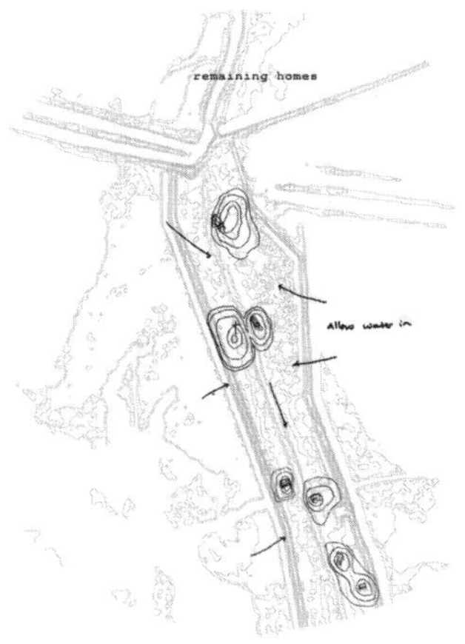

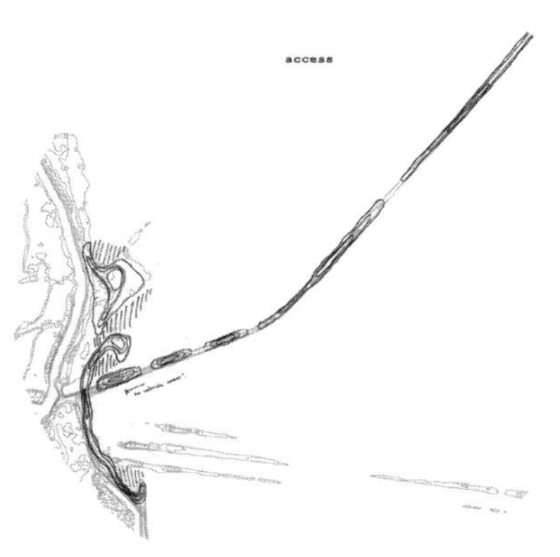

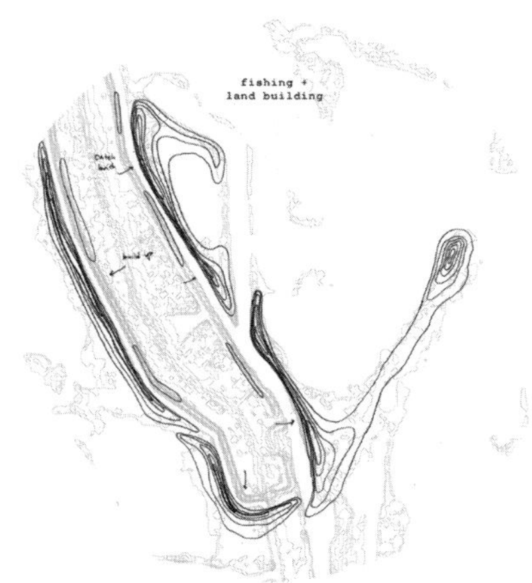

Opposite:
Isle de Jean Charles context.

Above:
Based on the spots known to have the best fishing, the families currently living on the island, and the location of the cemetery and the marina, these future landforms address possible desired goals of the community. These are thus an act of agency that, through the community's own understanding of the land and water divide, challenge the boundary drawn by the Army Corps.

Suggesting a design practice founded on social engagement and critical community knowledge, the act of landscape architecture here is a pre-emptive challenge to the arbitrary and objective land/water boundary placed on coastal landscapes. Beginning with the argument that such jurisdictional boundaries forget the memory and identity embedded in these local landscapes, Rise: A Guide to Boundary Resistance proposes continued, local and collective acts of boundary resistance in order to sustain communal agency and identity. Memory is our human connection to land, and is thus the product of our human desire to belong in space. The loss of land to the rising sea disrupts such connection with coastal lands and, therefore, the identity of the communities whose livelihoods depended on them. The loss of land is much more than the loss of soil. It is the loss of culture and place.

Central to the loss of ownership is the US Army Corps of Engineers' Ordinary High Water Mark (OHWM), which is used as a bureaucratic mechanism for state property ownership. For a steadily increasing number of coastal communities, this line on the map is not only constantly moving but also formed by physical characteristics on the ground that the Army Corps has determined divide private land and state-owned water. In the case of the Biloxi-Chitimacha-Choctaw tribe on the Isle de Jean Charles, Louisiana, this mark divides tribal and state properties. This Native American community, whose island has been cut up by the nearby oil industry, will be forced to leave for a landlocked parcel further north. They will eventually lose their island to the state as this water mark rises in the next 50 years.

However, if the water mark can be altered and obscured, the tribe will maintain ownership of their land even after they leave. Physical characteristics that the Army Corps uses to determine boundaries include the 'presence of litter and debris' and the 'destruction of terrestrial vegetation'; as such, the boundary is derived from the landscape according to the Corps' delineations. Thus, the project's guidebook outlines how each characteristic can be distorted to effectively challenge the OHWM and the property boundary it imposes. Explaining the nature of the water mark, who delineates it and their process of marking, the guide intends to give transparency to the act of boundary-making. Simultaneously, it imagines a cultural and generational undertaking of weekly and monthly actions that will ultimately transform the community's island.

In addition to these smaller-scale interventions, the project zooms out to find possible island forms. Based on the spots known to have the best fishing,

At the Isle de Jean Charles, land loss and constant flooding has forced many families to leave, with only 60 people left on the island out of the 300 residents that were once there. This is mostly due to the residents' lack of access to the mainland whenever the Island Road floods, restricting them from grocery stores, schools and hospitals.

Fisher Middle High School
Jean Lafitte Elementary School
Frank's Supermarket
Rouses
Pointe-Aux-Chenes Supermarket
Montegut Middle School
Price's Supermarket Inc
Montegut Elementary School
Isle de Jean Charles
60 residents
Frank's Supermarket

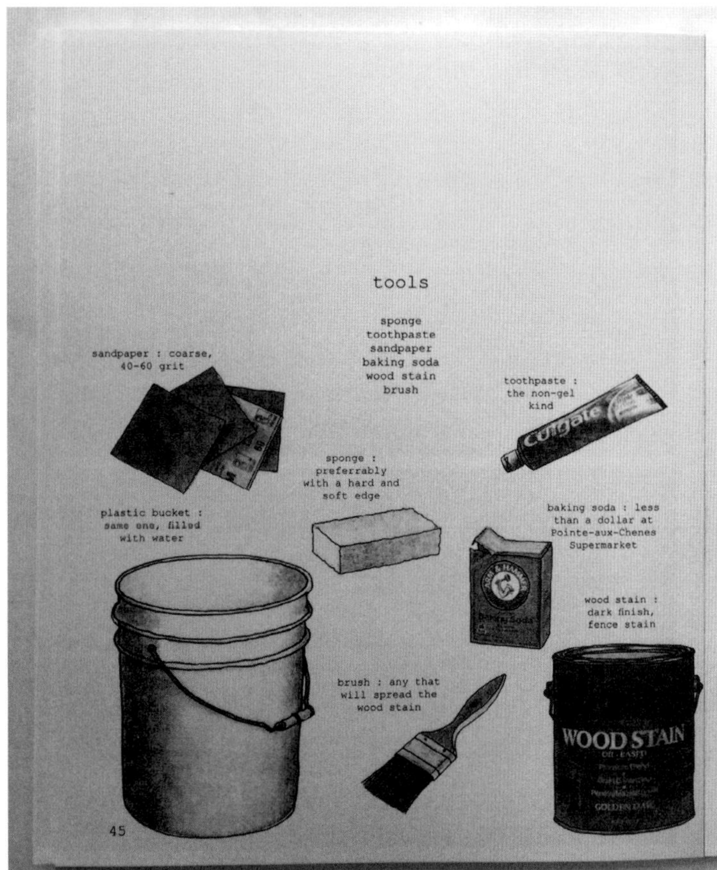

find

"staining or discoloring of natural or man-made objects due to the frequent presence of water."

With any boulders or wooden posts, frequent water inundation will have left a dark stain, leaving a clear indication of water's presence. You'll find these boulders all along the Island Road, and you'll find wooden posts supporting any bridges, signs in the water, or fishing docks. The Delineators use such clear marks as a way to measure the ordinary height of the water when no other clear Indicator is present onshore. They level the mark with the nearby land to project the mark there.

remove

If the mark is either gone or faked, the Delineators won't be able to tell which one to use! To remove the stain, mix an equal amount of baking soda and toothpaste in the bucket. The amount will depend on how much you're scrubbing off: usually 6" of stain will require 3 tablespoons of each. Scrub this mixture on the line and remove until there is a noticeable height difference in the water line. Even better, use sand paper after the mix dries to discolor it further.

fake

This will require a wood stain that is darker than the wood on the bridges and posts surrounding the island. With the brush, paint the stain significantly above (at least 2' higher) than the original mark. It should look much higher than the water level, so the Delineators could not possibly mistake it for the actual one.

46

the homes currently on the island, and the location of the island cemetery and marina, these future landforms address possible desired goals of the community. These forms do not attempt to save the entire island from rising sea levels, but they use community knowledge and understanding of the land the Biloxi-Chitimacha-Choctaw tribe have lived on for so long to maintain ownership and access to their waters.

The Guide to Boundary Resistance is not a project of preservation, but a project of autonomy that revisits what today's Native American culture looks like. The community's historic practices of gardening, burial and fishing remain connected to the island and relevant to their identities. In addition, it is a project of present-day Native American culture that is active in shaping Louisiana's landscape. The Guide to Boundary Resistance is grounded along the OHWM, but it is also active in pushing against the larger bureaucratic boundaries set up by the state and federal governments to control land for economic purposes. Through the community's persistent action along the imposed boundary line, the island is still their own. And, as a product, their identity as Biloxi-Chitimacha-Choctaw strengthens and continuously re-establishes as they shape their own land. Here, culture and landscape have a co-dependency that renders the land evermore present in our current conversation of political boundaries. Social formation is derived through landscape practices and, conversely, the land is formed by the memory and identities embedded in it.

The Guidebook to Boundary Resistance illustrates what to do to change the nature of the US Army Corps of Engineers' Ordinary High Water Mark (OHWM) and disrupt this superficial boundary, which is used as a bureaucratic mechanism for defining state property ownership. Explaining the nature of the water mark, who delineates it, and their process of marking, the guide intends to make such boundary-making transparent in order to effectively challenge it.

AILA
:
INDIGENOUS PERSPECTIVES ON AUSTRALIAN PROFESSIONAL LANDSCAPE PRACTICE SYMPOSIUM 2016

'Country' is a term used by Indigenous Australians to describe their significant and complex cultural connection to landscape. 'Connection to Country' provides a model for ecology and sustainability in which human care for landscape is intrinsic and meaningful. For landscape architects, seeing landscape through the lens of Country disrupts productively: it raises a series of questions about our opportunities and responsibilities when practicing on the Australian continent.

In recent years, the Australian Institute of Landscape Architecture (AILA) Victoria's Connection to Country Committee has advocated for a new paradigm of Australian professional landscape practice, one that recognises and incorporates Indigenous culture and knowledge systems. The committee formed as a result of momentum in the Victorian membership of AILA, and its primary focus since has been the development of a Connection to Country Strategy for the Institute's Victorian chapter. This strategy seeks to actively engage with Indigenous communities, increase members' knowledge of Victorian Indigenous culture and embed this knowledge into the teaching and practice of landscape architecture. The committee has also drafted the base for a national Reconciliation Action Plan, to make the proposals of this strategy actionable and measurable.

In partnership with the City of Melbourne and Indigenous Architecture and Design Victoria, the committee led a one-day symposium that launched a discourse amongst the state chapter by drawing together the perspectives and knowledge of local Victorian Aboriginal collaborators. The committee's work has catalysed a discussion at the national level of the Institute, with a recently nominated nationwide Connection to Country committee and further development of the Reconciliation Action Plan currently taking shape.

The March 2016 Connection to Country symposium featured an all-Indigenous panel of speakers who explored the translation of a Connection to Country approach to professional design practice, and was the first of its kind in Australia.

The event's nine speakers included Bill Nicholson, Reuben Berg, Paul Paton, James Hackel, Jefa Greenaway, Vicki Couzens, Timmah Ball and Alan Titchener. The speakers represented diverse disciplinary backgrounds – two artists, a cultural consultant, a planner, a language specialist, a landscape architect, a park management planner and two architects. Their perspectives informed the varied principles and advice they shared on respectful cultural engagement. Their words address fundamental concepts and values as well as practical processes and resources.

– AILA Victoria Connection to Country Committee

On defining Country and connection to Country

Bill Nicholson

1. Bird Rose, D 2004, Reports from a Wild Country: Ethics for Decolonisation, UNSW Press, Sydney.

Bill Nicholson is a Wurundjeri Elder whose grandmother was born at Coranderrk in 1914 and who also has connections to Dja Dja Wurrung and Taungurung people. Uncle Bill is an expert cultural consultant and is currently the Education and Research Manager at the Wurundjeri Land Council.

A map of languages reveals that Aboriginal Australia is more multicultural than Europe, with hundreds of languages and 600–700 different dialects. Each group has their own customs, beliefs, ceremonies and language and their own connection to Country. There is cultural information that is specific to an area and the boundaries of cultural and language groups are usually defined by landscape types.

There is a physical and a spiritual connection to Country. The physical connection is basically the utilisation of resources in a sustainable manner. The spiritual connection is deeper than that. Even after you pass away, your spirit can still reside on your land. Your connection to Country never actually ends, which makes it the strongest connection possible. It is important to respect the culture and land on which you do business, and to acknowledge Elders. Find out which Country you're living on. Find out the history of the land where you live – and understand it.

With Indigenous people forming less than three per cent of the population in Victoria, non-Indigenous communities and individuals must do more to care for the land and Country. Half the land in Aboriginal Victoria is under ownership or dispute of some kind. Boundaries should not divide, but bring people together; boundaries are formed through stories and cultural recognition. This is also a potentially respectful and productive approach between Indigenous and non-Indigenous cultures, as well as within Indigenous Victoria.

On Traditional Ownership of Country

Reuben Berg

Rueben Berg is a Gunditjmara man, and is the executive officer, and a co-founder, of Indigenous Architecture and Design Victoria, a not-for-profit organisation which aims to strengthen culture and design in the built environment.

There are more than thirty-seven different Aboriginal groups in Victoria and the way that people connect to these diverse groups varies widely. An individual may have connections to a single group, or to a number of groups. Who speaks and who has the authority to speak on behalf of a particular group is often not a straightforward matter. All of this can be overwhelming for those seeking to engage.

There are three main representative structures. The first is the Traditional Owner Settlement Act 2010. This Act provides for an out-of-court settlement of native title and delivery of land justice. The Traditional Owner Settlement Act allows the Victorian Government to make agreements to recognise Traditional Owners and their rights in Crown land, in return for agreement to withdraw all current native title claims and not to lodge any claims in the future.

Registered Aboriginal Parties (RAP) operate in relation to the Victorian Aboriginal Heritage Act 2006, which recognises Aboriginal people as the primary guardians, keepers and knowledge-holders of Aboriginal cultural heritage. RAPs are the voice of Aboriginal people in the management and protection of Aboriginal cultural heritage in Victoria.

RAP responsibilities under the Act include evaluating Cultural Heritage Management Plans, providing advice on applications for Cultural Heritage Permits, making decisions about Cultural Heritage Agreements and providing advice or application for interim or ongoing Protection Declarations.

There are currently ten RAPs in Victoria, which cover about sixty per cent of the state, but in many places it is unclear who the RAP is. There is ongoing discussion around where the boundaries lie between different groups, or which group should represent those areas.

Non-Traditional Owner groups include co-ops, health services, youth services and local community organisations. Such groups are not necessarily Traditional Owners, and may encompass people with a range of cultural affiliations.

Ownership can be an emotive issue, and many Aboriginal people are passionate about who is identified as the Traditional Owner, and who deserves recognition and representation. Navigating this space can be very difficult, but is worthwhile if done in the right way.

On language, culture and Country

Paul Paton

Paul Paton is a Gunai and Monaro man and is the executive officer of the Victorian Aboriginal Corporation for Languages (VACL). Paul has over fourteen years of experience working with Aboriginal communities around Victoria and working with government departments in the area of language, policy and curriculum.

Language is culture; culture is language. Languages are crucial to Country and identity, and are repositories of knowledge. For example, songlines helped guide Aboriginal people through their Country. Dreaming trails have a memory function, and work to teach the layout of the land and its names. In turn, place names teach the Dreaming story, articulating what happened where.

Language is a principal means to know kinship, relationships and place in the community. When we start getting our languages back, we know who we are and where we come from – and we know where we want to go.

Sadly, Aboriginal culture has little visibility in the urban environment. Place names are just one way that Aboriginal culture can be brought to the fore and shared with the general community. When seeking to use the names of Country and language, it is important to be cognizant of the complexities and respectful of the local communities. It is essential to seek advice, do appropriate background research, and follow local protocols, which provide a dynamic guide to the use of language in particular places.

- Use community-accepted spellings (in some cases there may be more than one accepted spelling).
- Be aware that language changes over time, and sometimes spellings and pronunciation will revert back to older preferences as part of the language reclamation journey.
- Know and understand local protocols. Recognise that these will differ between communities, and can change over time.
- Talk to communities at the beginning of the process, not at the end, and recognise that consultation takes time.

On collaborative landscape management

James Hackel

James Hackel is a Palawa man whose Aboriginal heritage is from Tasmania. He has a Bachelor of Landscape Architecture from RMIT University and joined Parks Victoria in 2001. James has worked with several Aboriginal communities across Victoria on cultural heritage projects and Traditional Owner engagement. His involvement in the development of management plans for some of Victoria's most significant national parks aims to recognise the unique cultural context and complexity of Indigenous politics.

There are many opportunities when working with people who have a very strong connection and understanding of their connection to Country. It is important to engage with Aboriginal groups and to respect the legitimacy of Country.

Parks Victoria takes a regional landscape approach to management planning. This involves developing management plans for sixteen landscape areas. This accords with the International Union for the Conservation of Nature (IUCN), which identifies a landscape scale approach as best practice, and aligns with other contemporary planning approaches in Victoria, such as fire and natural resource management. This landscape-wide, multi-tenure approach ensures a consistent management approach across multiple parks. The fifteen year timeframe enables a strategic approach to the use of tight resources and is a more efficient scale for engaging community, stakeholders and Traditional Owners.

Parks Victoria works with Registered Aboriginal Parties (RAPs) as identifying distinct areas is complex politically – as soon as a line is drawn on a map it can be disputed – and it is critical to know who the right people are, and know that they have the authority to speak for Country.

There are currently two modes of collaborative management – joint management and co-management. For either to be in place the relevant Aboriginal corporations need to have governance processes and certainty of status as the representatives of Country. Joint management by Parks Victoria and Traditional Owners is described by Parks Victoria as:

> A formal partnership arrangement between Traditional Owners and the State where both share their knowledge to manage specific national parks and other protected areas. Joint management recognises the ongoing connection of Traditional Owners to the land. It involves Traditional Owners and park staff sharing their knowledge to manage specific areas.

The certainty of status that this confers on Traditional Owners is empowering, and brings the aspirations of Traditional Owners to light. Co-management is another form of partnership, and is an outcome of the recognition of Native Title. Under this arrangement, title to parks and reserves is not transferred to the Traditional Owners, but they shape the ongoing management of specific parks by forming councils with representatives from Parks Victoria, the Department of Environment and Primary Industries and Catchment Management Authorities.

On deep listening and Aboriginal architecture

Jefa Greenaway

Jefa Greenaway is an award-winning architect and interior designer. Jefa is director of the boutique design practice Greenaway Architects and Chair of the not-for-profit organisation Indigenous Architecture and Design Victoria (IADV). As the first and only registered Indigenous architect in Victoria, he has demonstrated a commitment to embedding cultural connectedness within the built environment. A recipient of the prestigious AIA Dulux Study Tour – Emerging Architect Prize, he champions design leadership in practice and academia. He is a member of the City of Melbourne's Public Art Advisory Panel and Art Lab Curatorium.

Aboriginal people have the oldest continuous culture in the world – it is something to be proud of, and an experience to be shared. When working on projects, it is important to reference some of these connections to culture wherever possible.

A series of important connections needs to be made when working within the built environment. Dialogue, research and collaboration are very important. Professionals who operate in the built environment need to park their ego at the door because invariably there are a lot of things that are unknown and must be explored. The only way to do this is through deep listening – consultation, collaboration and participation. With any project that relates to Aboriginal communities, it is important to acknowledge connections to history and memory, and to understand that there are always cultural considerations that underpin the design. It is not always a linear process.

People often ask what Aboriginal architecture is. It is architecture by, for and with Aboriginal people. It is inextricably linked to connection to Country. The starting point is always to understand the location and to reference that place, to tell those stories and to embed those narratives, and to weave them subtly into the projects. Aspects that are not typical of mainstream projects require engagement. This may be social justice, employment and ceremonial aspects of the project.

On cultural reclamation, reconcilation and respectful relationship-building

Vicki Couzens

Vicki Couzens is a Keerray Wurrong woman from the Western Districts of Victoria. Vicki has worked in Aboriginal community affairs for over thirty-five years. She is a senior knowledge holder for Possum Skin Cloak Story and Language Reclamation and Revival in her Gunditjmara Mother Tongue. Vicki's contributions in the reclamation, regeneration and revitalisation of cultural knowledge and practices extend across the arts and cultural expression spectrum including language research and community development, public art, community arts, visual and performing arts, writing, publications and her own creative expression. Vicki acknowledges her Ancestors and Elders who guide her in her work.

Aboriginal culture can be described through two words, respect and relationship. These words encompass big concepts and principles. Respect is listening, responsibility and acknowledgement. The law of the land is living and each person is connected in the great web of life.

Indigenous artists working across different communities must follow appropriate protocols and processes, just as non-Indigenous people must do, and recognise that the dynamics of engagement and relationships can change over time. It is important to recognise the sensitivity of working on another people's Country and it is not appropriate for artists from elsewhere – including Indigenous artists – to simply bring their stories to this site. Artists must navigate all of this. They must build respectful relationships and be conscious of the law of the land that determines your place and who you are. They must understand they are standing on the shoulders of others and being guided by the old people, by ancestors and family, by Country.

On integrating Indigenous culture in the urban built environment

Timmah Ball

Timmah grew up in Melbourne but her heritage, on her mother's side, is Ballardong Noongar from Western Australia. Timmah is passionate about using arts and culture to create inclusive cities, and believes that planners need to think about people rather than zones and overlays. Her writing has appeared in Inflection Journal, Right Now and Etchings Indigenous, and she is a regular contributor to Assemble Papers.

Urban planning and architecture are forms of colonisation. Robert Hoddle marks the Melbourne grid at the same time as Aboriginal culture and history is erased. Paul Fox, the urban historian, looks at the process of colonisation and asks us, 'do we want to see images of Paris or London or New York when we walk around our major cities, or do we want to create our own sense of design?' If non-Aboriginal Australians are asking such questions, then Aboriginal people are even more deeply concerned with finding ways to share our culture and to strengthen it in the built environment. Aboriginal artists and writers have been looking at this for a long time now.

Writer Tony Birch makes strong arguments for new ways of conceptualising Indigenous Australia – 'There is a narrowness contained in white Australia's construction of Indigenous culture. We need to find new ways of looking at ourselves.'[2] Ellen van Neerven positions Aboriginal culture as a strategy to tackle issues of sustainability in our cities – 'Greater understanding and application of Aboriginal and Torres Straight Islander knowledge and practice will help with future challenges'. Academic planners argue that we need to challenge technical bureaucratic approaches to the built environment: 'Planning that ignores diverse ways of knowing undermines the experiences and shared meaning of those living in a city.'[3]

We need to move away from the scientific modernism embedded in things like zones and overlays. Modern cities are complex and fractured places. We need to find new ways to solve our problems, new ways to find out who we are and to plan for our future.

Aboriginal artists explore the preservation and currency of Aboriginal culture through works that engage with the contemporary city and its histories, and remind us that Melbourne's inner suburbs have a strong significance as meeting places for Indigenous people. There is some fantastic work now being done to strengthen Aboriginal culture in the built environment – and the next step is to continue the discussion around how we can create inclusive cities and how we can ensure that a range of voices are being heard and represented in our cities.

2. Birch, T 2005, Black On White, Centre for Contemporary Photography

3. Goldstein, BE, Taufen-Wessells, A, Lejano, R & Butler, W 2013, Narrating resilience: Transforming urban systems through collaborative storytelling, Urban Studies 52(7).

On the translation of indigenous cultural connection to landscape professional practice in New Zealand

Alan Titchener

Alan Titchener is of Ngai Tahu descent and is a senior member of the landscape architecture profession in New Zealand. He is a past president and Fellow of the New Zealand Institute of Landscape Architects and is a past president of the Asia-Pacific Region of the International Federation of Landscape Architects. He is a founding member and Pae Matua (Senior) member of Nga Aho (a multidisciplinary collective of Maori Design Professionals) and was recently accorded Kahui Whetu status by that group. Alan has a special interest in Te Ao Māori(Māori World View) as it pertains to landscape architecture and is a passionate advocate for the recognition and incorporation of Māori values in the practice and teaching of landscape architecture.

The Māori belief system is based on the concept of the interrelatedness of people with the living and nonliving elements of nature. It is a societal model based on *Whakapapa* (genealogy) and *Whanaungatanga* (kinship and networks). The belief system includes, among many other concepts: *Mana* – responsibility for particular areas of land; *Rangatiratanga* – good decision making; *Tikanga* – the protocols by which people live their lives, expressed through narrative; *Kotahitanga* – unity, oneness, interconnectedness and the need to make decisions collectively.

All Māori landscape architects are trained in Western education systems, and must find ways to draw the Māori belief system into this model.

In 2007 a collective of Māori design professionals established the formal organisation, Nga Aho, based on earlier informal associations. This was the first time that seventy Māori design and built environments professionals had come together. The following year saw Te Tau-a-Nuku, the Māori Landscape Architects group, form.

Nga Aho developed the Te Aranga Māori Cultural Landscape Strategy. Drawn up by Māori to articulate Māori interests and aspirations in the built environment, it was grounded in concepts of place and belonging and articulated the Māori wish to make their culture a visible and integral part of the future of Aotearoa/New Zealand. It argued that successful design allows Māori to see themselves reflected in their natural environments, places of work, leisure, urban environments and residences. The framework for the strategy was threefold: *Mana* (to empower), *Matauranga* (to inform) and *Rawa* (to equip).

The strategy is summed up in the following statements.

As Māori we have a unique sense of our 'landscape'.

- It includes past, present and future.
- It includes both physical and spiritual dimensions.
- It is how we express ourselves in our environment.
- It connects *whanau* and *whenua*, flora and fauna, through *whakapapa*.
- It does not disconnect urban from rural.
- It transcends the boundaries of 'land'scape into other 'scapes': rivers, lakes, ocean and sky.
- It is enshrined in our *whakapapa*, *pepeha* (tribal saying), *tauparapara* (incantation to begin a speech), *whaikorero* (formal speeches), *karakia* (ritual chants), *waiata* (speeches), *tikanga* (correct procedure, custom, lore, method), *nga korero a kui ma*, a *koroua ma* (the words of our elders), and our *mahi toi* (art and architecture).
- It is not just where we live – it is who we are!

In 2010 Auckland Council was formed through the amalgamation of eight territorial authorities. This was an opportunity to embed the Te Aranga Strategy in the form of a set of design principles. This includes seven outcome-oriented design principles:

Mana – recognition of *Mana Whenua* and the outcome of relationships expressed
Whakapapa – relevant Māori names are expressed
Tohu – broader cultural landscape markers are acknowledged
Taiao – native/vernacular landscapes are promoted/restored/enhanced
Mauri Tu – environmental health is promoted/restored/enhanced
Mahi Toi – narratives are expressed artistically and with integrity
Aki Kaa – a space and place for *Mana Whenua* to engage and flourish

Embedding these principles is a significant step in terms of recognising and embracing Te Ao Māori. The Auckland City Design Office is a staunch advocate and recently appointed a key member of Nga Aho and Te Tau-a-Nuku to champion these principles.

Acknowledgments:

The Connection to Country Committee would like to acknowledge the generous support of the AILA Victoria Executive Committee and Chapter Office. During this two-year term, the chapter and its executive team have made the Connection to Country Strategy one of its key strategic initiatives and endorsed the Connection to Country Symposium as the chapter's major event of the 2016 calendar year.

The committee thanks the City of Melbourne and Indigenous Architecture and Design Victoria, who partnered with the committee to realise the symposium.

Mandy Nicholson, Wurundjeri artist, is also thanked for generously presenting, leading public art tours and participating in panel discussion at the symposium.

The committee also thanks Justine Carey for producing an extensive written record of the symposium, which makes this article possible and which is available in full on the AILA website as a booklet edited by Lauren Gillard: www.aila.org.au

GRANT REVELL

:

SO YOU WANT(ED) TO BE A (DISRUPTIVE) LANDSCAPE ARCHITECT?

> We were talking about the love that's gone so cold. And the people who gain the world and lose their soul. They don't know, they can't see, are you one of them?[1]

It is hard to imagine twenty five editions of disruptive Kerb, yet I was there at the very beginning as a design teacher, to help (re)invent and share a new landscape architecture, from the far west of Australia. We were inspired by the intellectual tenacities and somewhat recklessness of our RMIT colleagues. Kerb was refreshing and illuminating, and we knew that we had something special to contribute.

For a while we kept to our entitled selves. Our former eastern leadership was genius. Old roots went deep, and Marion Blackwell kept us suitably honest. Fortunately, our disruptive student bodies were also certain about their misbehaviours. They were inspirational. Every day it seemed we were collectively redefining the psyche of our collaborative landscapes. We were on a roll, and yes, we secretly knew it. It was so often politically charged and mostly disruptive – it was experimental – just like the inter-subjectivities of landscape itself. Yet, this time 'landscape' was somehow developing a voice of its own. Pascoe, Lines, Berry, Benterrak, Muecke and Roe, Ghirri, Tacey, Morgan, and Mowaljarlai, certainly helped.[2]

Our geo-cultural and raconteur-type language was rapidly changing, and it was timely to write, draw and have a yarn about what we knew, and felt, of this new landscape design thinking. Whilst many stood (awkwardly) tall in the urban hallways, others took up the invite to head to the bush (and its wellbeing). For the most, we were pretty much left alone and that sweet absence was important for it allowed a centred disruption. It certainly wasn't exotic as others contested. Of course, it was (and remains) mean ol' Western Australia – a deeply provincial and racist place – with or without its enticing and ancient design ecologies.

In all the glorious uncertainty of Kerb Journal there was one standout article that has had a profound impact on my teachings and me. This influential article – 'Landscape and remembering: the world, the earth and their strife' – was from RMIT, by social anthropologist Gerard Gill.[3] It remains revelatory for me as it helps explain Australian landscape, in the context of practicing landscape architecture as a much deeper expression of societal ill-health, or 'strife' as it is known. A contested cultural barometer within its own foreign otherness I thought – an uncertain cultural measurement, or litmus of truth and practiced reason.

I have explained this article's importance in other Kerb articles and it still sticks with me as one of my southern stars. For many non-indigenous people of Australia, I think it opens up questions that still need exploring (more than ever

1. Harrison, G 1967, Within you without you, Capitol Records, California.

2. Pascoe, B 1986, Night Animals, Penguin, Ringwood, Victoria; Benterrak, K, Muecke, S & Roe, P 1984, Reading the Country: Introduction to Nomadology, Fremantle Arts Centre Press, Fremantle, Western Australia; Lines, WJ 1991, Taming the Great South Land: A History of the Conquest of Nature in Australia, Allen & Unwin, North Sydney, NSW; Berry, T 1988, The Dream of the Earth, Sierra Club Books, San Francisco; Ghirri, L 1978, Kodachrome, 2nd edn, MACK, London; Tacey, D 1992, 'Dreaming our myths onwards', Island, no.53, pp. 58-62; Morgan, S 1988, My Place: An Australian Classic, Fremantle Press, North Fremantle, Western Australia; Mowaljarlai, D & Malnic, J 1993, Yorro yorro = Everything Standing Up Alive: Spirit of the Kimberley, Magabala Books, Broome, Western Australia.

perhaps) – and these are:

- How do we learn or transform landscape into country without taking away anything Indigenous?
- How do we best landscape architecturalise a knowing of endemic country rather than foreign landscape?
- And in the process how do we decolonise many of our unethical histories of being?
- How do we collectively and genuinely liberate these ethical transformations of Australia by the determined capacities of an Indigenous voice?

For students of landscape architecture education and practice these questions are hopefully more relevant and meaningful today than they were when Kerb first started in 1992. Perhaps not.

Meanwhile, I was well and truly committed to a reciprocal relationship with my fellow Indigenous colleagues. I had long begun my 'unlearning' of knowing relational cultural landscapes. Of course, from most bush invites I had no choice. It soon became my grounded in-between, for experiential landscape learning and teaching. Two worlds were colliding. We were all students. The novelties of grounded theory in sociology were evolving.[4]

Others, including myself, were sidetracked by Simon Swaffield's desperate call for a unifying landscape strategy, but we knew it would never quite make sense for a deliriously heterogeneous discipline to be sandwiched between multiple worlds.[6] Especially a mostly fragile discipline that would so often make a living by turning its back on Indigenous cultures. For the time being it just had to be grounded and made real. But we knew it had to have an Indigenous voice.[7]

It is worth reminding ourselves that Australian landscape architecture, as both a discipline and profession (with few exceptions), essentially still remains a set of colonial practices. It clearly privileges dominant white western ideologies and ways of 'knowing, being and doing' Australia.[8] It is mostly derived from a strange otherness of dominance, power and control. It often compels a functional, technical and poetic use of borrowed land and water to justify the cross-cultural identities and livelihoods of subsequent non-Indigenous Australians. There are few independent exceptions to these contested practices other than within the place-worlds of many of Australia's Indigenous owners.

Many efforts of landscape architecture have, for the most part, avoided genuine partnerships with Indigenous knowledge custodians. Our individual and collective abilities to liberate Indigenous self-determination, and encourage social and economic capacity-building for Indigenous peoples, have failed us miserably. Why is this so? Why do so many landscape architects simply avoid these professional responsibilities and obligations?

Of course, this question of professional and everyday uncertainty is not new to Kerb. It was in fact, one of the key intellectual pillars to its own disruptive gestation way back when Melbourne's LA Edge Conference helped define its earlier charter in the early 80s. It was a wakeup call that still resonates among many of its founders. We should be ever thankful for the sustained efforts of Jerry de Gryse and Maggie Fooke. I was fortunate to be one of their foot soldiers. Above all, those critical moments in Australian landscape architectural history clearly understood Australian landscape as a deeply troubled social construct – a disturbing Anthropocene well ahead of its time. But it wasn't 'site' (beauty, loss of biodiversity or climate change) that dominated its discourse – it was relational being; embodied presence. Without ourselves or our landscape associations we were nothing. Edge seriously pushed the buttons for all those that participated in that conference – where de Gryse and Fooke teased it out of us, to make the responsible intellectual leap into those neighbouring Indigenous worlds. And at that time, they clearly Indigenised the seemingly risky and humanised conversation of university design education. It was rambunctious. It was healthy.

Today, challenges remain with higher education in landscape architecture. The sector is now held responsible to perform alongside our Indigenous partners, and explicitly spell out the professional learning game plan for 2017-2020. The Universities of Australia's Indigenous Education Strategy invites all partner universities, and their agencies, to 'become the change makers required to produce substantive outcomes for Aboriginal and Torres Strait Islander people and the Australian nation.'[9]

It is worth summarising the current nation-wide commitments of the Indigenous Strategy, and considering where and how our landscape architectural education and professional institutions could play an active role in these worthy initiatives:

- maintain institutional growth rates for Aboriginal and Torres Strait Islander peoples' enrolment of at least 50 per cent above the growth rate of non-Indigenous student enrolment, and ideally 100 per cent above;
- aim for retention and success rates for Aboriginal and Torres Strait Islander students equal to those of domestic non-Indigenous students, in the same fields of study by 2025;
- aim to achieve equal completion rates by field of study by 2028;
- include Indigenous higher education, research and employment as priority areas in core policy documents, including institutional strategic and business plans;
- have Indigenous Research Strategies in place by 2018;
- ensure that implementation of these plans and policies is devolved through the university's faculties, schools and units;

3. Gill, G 2001, 'Landscape and remembering: the world, the earth and their strife', Kerb: Journal of Landscape Architecture, no.10, pp. 34-37

4. Swaffield, S 2002, Theory in Landscape Architecture: a Reader, University of Pennsylvania Press, Philadelphia.

5. Ibid

6. Our knowledge, our land, Ngalang Kaadadjan, Ngalang Boodja 2017, 'Story Threads', <http://www.ourknowledgeourland.com.au/gallery/art-collection/>.

7. Strauss, A & Juliet, C 1994, 'Grounded theory methodology: an overview', in N. Denzin & Y. Lincoln (eds), Handbook of qualitative research, Vol.1, pp. 273–284.

8. Martin, KL 2008, Please knock before you enter: Aboriginal regulation of outsiders and the implications for researchers, Post Pressed, Teneriffe, Queensland.

9. Universities of Australia 2017, Indigenous Strategy 2017-2020, Universities Australia, Canberra, ACT.

10. Ibid, p.9.

11. Ibid, p.14.

12. Ibid, p.2.

- ensure that additional workload expected of Aboriginal and Torres Strait Islander staff is recognised in workload planning and in performance assessments and promotions processes;
- build robust, respectful and collaborative partnerships between the institution and the Aboriginal and Torres Strait Islander communities that they serve;
- take a community leadership role in promoting Indigenous higher education, and building opportunities for wider community engagement in it;
- have current executive staff and all new senior staff complete cross-cultural training programs from 2018; and
- have processes that ensure all students will encounter and engage with Aboriginal and Torres Strait Islander cultural content as an integral part of their course of study, by 2020.[11]

These are big commitments, and as we collectively unwrap landscape into country we will need to suitably encourage and make space for the leadership of more Indigenous landscape architects (or their equivalent). Supporting and liberating ways of listening to and promoting Indigenous voices in decision making that affects Indigenous communities, and their lands and waters, remains our greatest challenge. Meanwhile, as opportunities for Indigenous education justifiably increase, hopefully the creative arts and industries of design culture will again prosper – where university campuses are clearly recognised and designed as traditional Indigenous places of higher community teaching, learning and research and where inclusive place-based storytelling and Indigenised curricula is strengthened within the social and emotional wellbeing of these animated landscapes and their traditional owners.

As noted in the strategy, 'It is important to remind ourselves that this vast lineage of educators spanned more than 2500 generations before Australia's first university was designated formally 166 years ago.'[12] Highly experiential, these reclaimed landscapes will have the ongoing potential for Indigenous landscape architects and their communities to heal and self-determine their knowledge systems and every-day cultural livelihoods by design.

Finally, I trust Kerb and many of its followers can continue to address these justifiable goals for another twenty five editions.

WORLDWEBOALLOTHING

WORLDWEBOALLOTHING

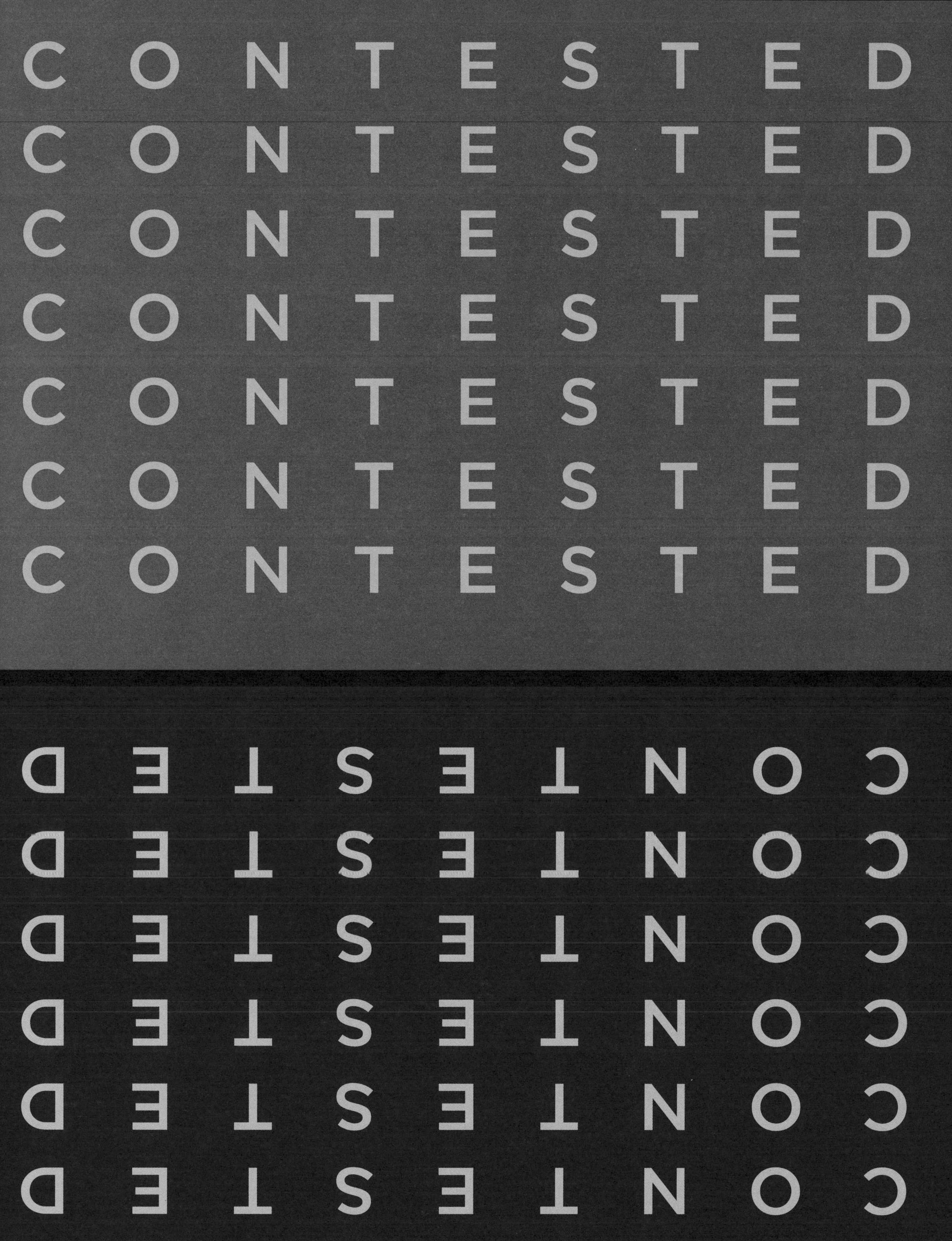
C O N T E S T E D
C O N T E S T E D
C O N T E S T E D
C O N T E S T E D
C O N T E S T E D
C O N T E S T E D
C O N T E S T E D

Asa
Kremmer

ATLAS OF BORDERS: UNPACKING THE ROLE OF THE CARTOGRAPHER

'The world is complex, dynamic, and multidimensional; the paper is static, flat. How are we to represent the rich visual world of experience and measurement on mere flatland?'
Edward R Tufte[1]

Approach

As cartography can tell us, the map as a design tool implies meaning and sets out new relationships.[2] This process of drawing understands the importance of revealing the larger geographic, political, economic and social relationships that manifest on the landscape. As a result, the map declares and is not impartial, but rather entails the cartographer's vision, conjecture and ability to set up new realities.

One of these realities that I am testing is the extent of the colonial map and its offset lines – an exhaustive cartographic catastrophe – as a tool to demarcate walls, fences, checkpoints, and divide people, places and identity. In many cases maps led to the dispossession of land and the displacement of entire communities.[3]

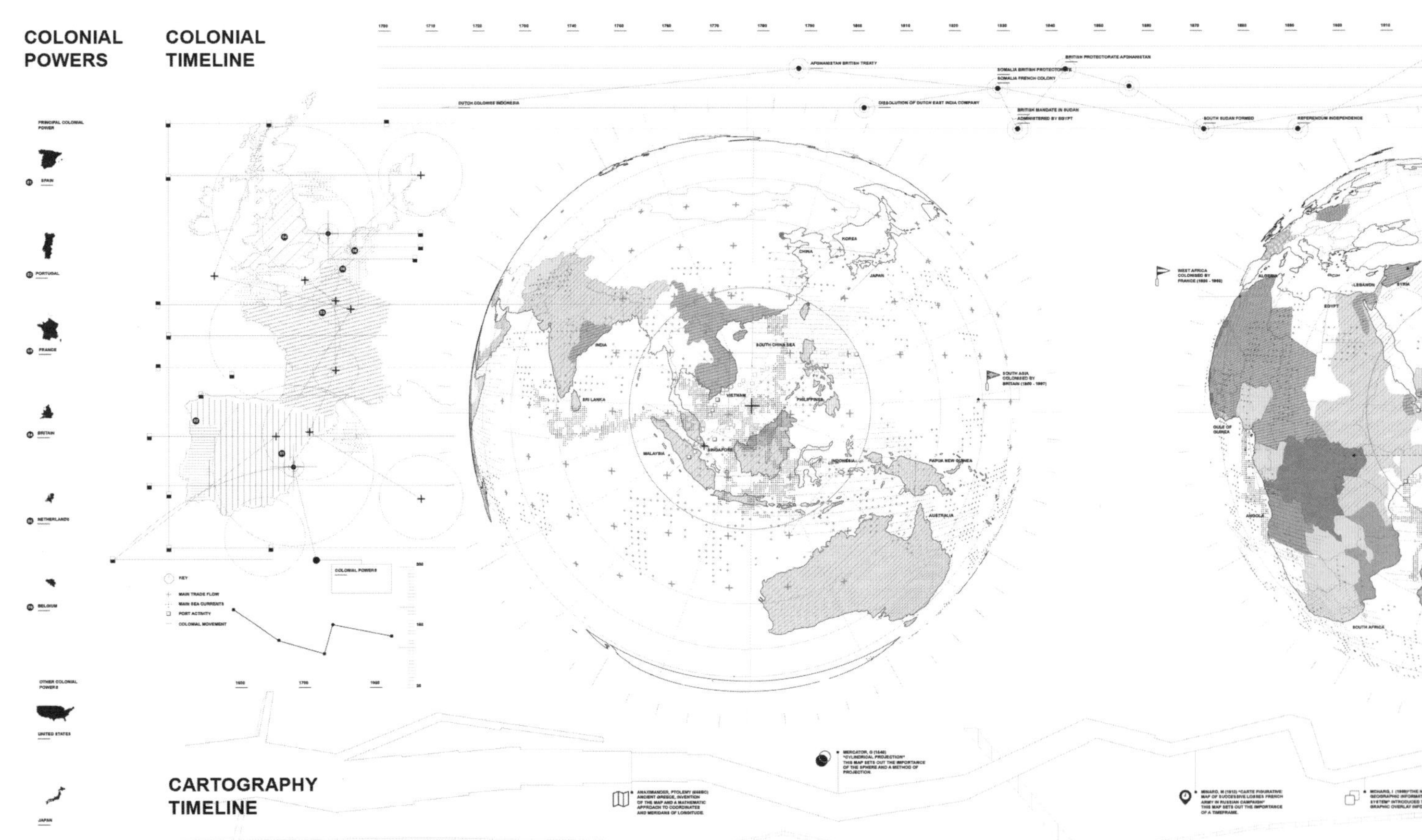

Mapping Colonialism
A historical mapping of colonial territories (British, French, Dutch, Spanish, Portuguese, Belgium)

1. Tufte, E 1990, Envisioning Information, 6th edn, Graphic Press, Cheshire, England.

2. Corner, J 1999, 'The agency of mapping: speculation, critique and invention', in Cosgrove, D (ed.), Mappings, Reaktion Books, London, United Kingdom.

3. Hardt, M & Negri, A 2000, Empire, Harvard University Press, Cambridge, Massachusetts, United States.

4. Houtum, H, Kramsch, O & Zierhofer, W 2005 (eds), 'Prologue', in Wasti-Walter, D (ed.), B/ordering space, Ashgate, Aldershot, England, pp. 1-13.

5. Tufte, E 1990, Envisioning Information, 6th edn, Graphic Press, Cheshire, England.

In the future, displacement will also occur from rising sea levels, and homelands may possibly disappear entirely in the South Pacific. Our relationship (as a direct result of colonial prosperity) to these shifting territories is central to Australia's sociopolitical direction and to ensuring those at risk of becoming climate refugees are not left more vulnerable.

This calls for a new scale.

Territory scale

The territory scale stretches across the projection of the map to copy the features of the globe onto a curved shape that you can cut open or lay flat (this shape, a sphere, sets up the suggestion of movement and more importantly human conditions).

Border scale

The fixed border reacts to this process as a collection of these circumstances. It performs as a type of catchment, buffer and aperture.

In most cases the mode of border entry is fundamental. If the legitimacy of entry (due to safety or lawfulness) is questioned, the individual or group will be denied entry. This may, however, entrap disadvantaged people within a kind of catchment area to become contained - held in waiting. Some of these spaces occur between multiple territories - a buffer that demarcates two or more powers - for example, the Rukban border between Jordan, Iraq and Syria, with its earthen berms.[4]

If an aperture is present then movement through a checkpoint is seized.

Outcome

These operations extract evidence from landscape conditions and cartography conventions, and propose a new form of drawing at multiple scales, in order to shift the pictorial and therefore aid the role of cartographer. Not only does this oppose mere flatland, but alludes to the multidimensional spatial conditions, so that the map can uncover the Z-axis that lies hidden in the paper.[5]

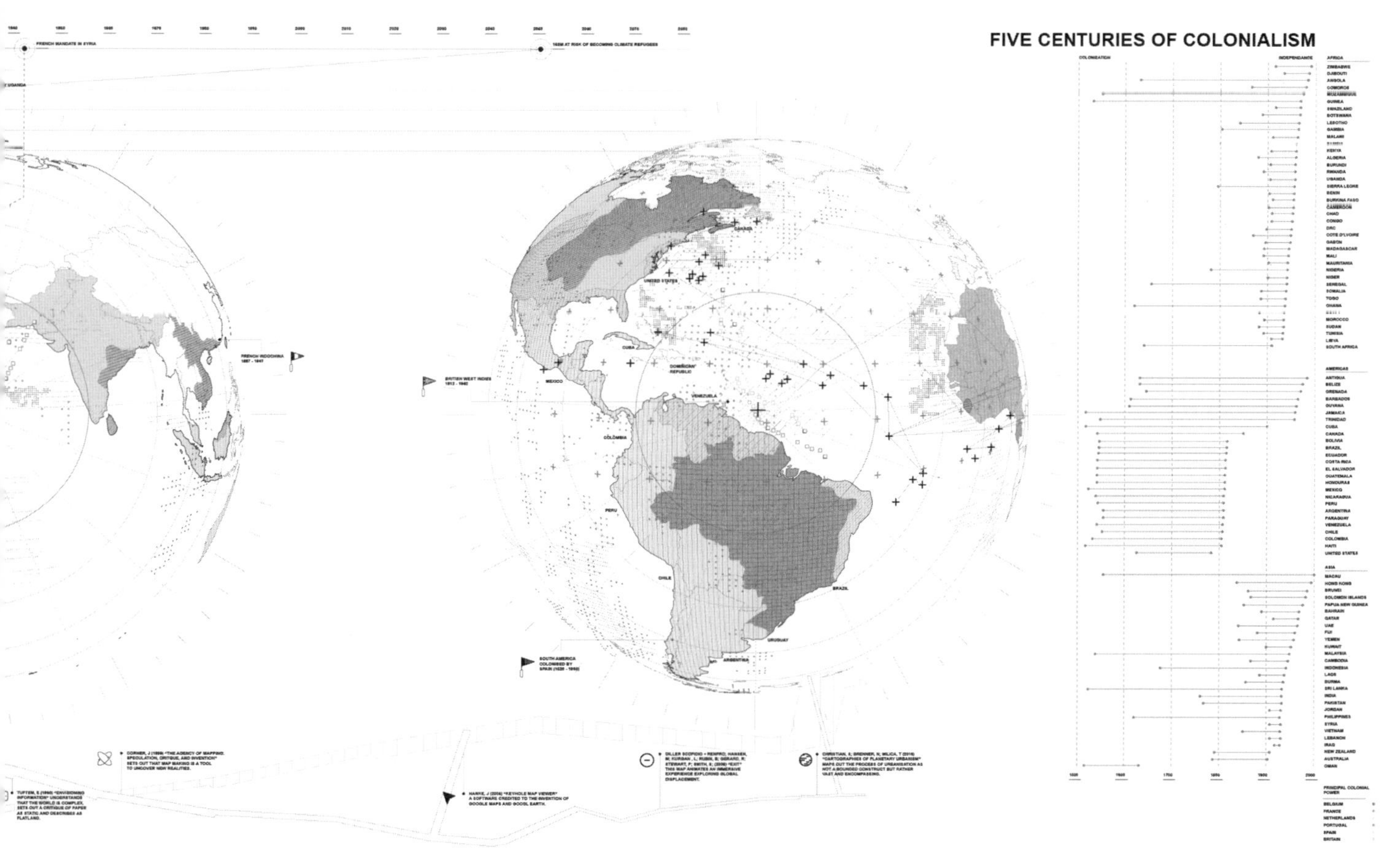

MARITIME BORDERS

Expanding the territory scale
The territory scale stretches across the projection of the map to copy the features of the globe onto a curved shape - a sphere – that you can cut open or lay flat (this shape sets up the suggestion of movement and more importantly human conditions.)

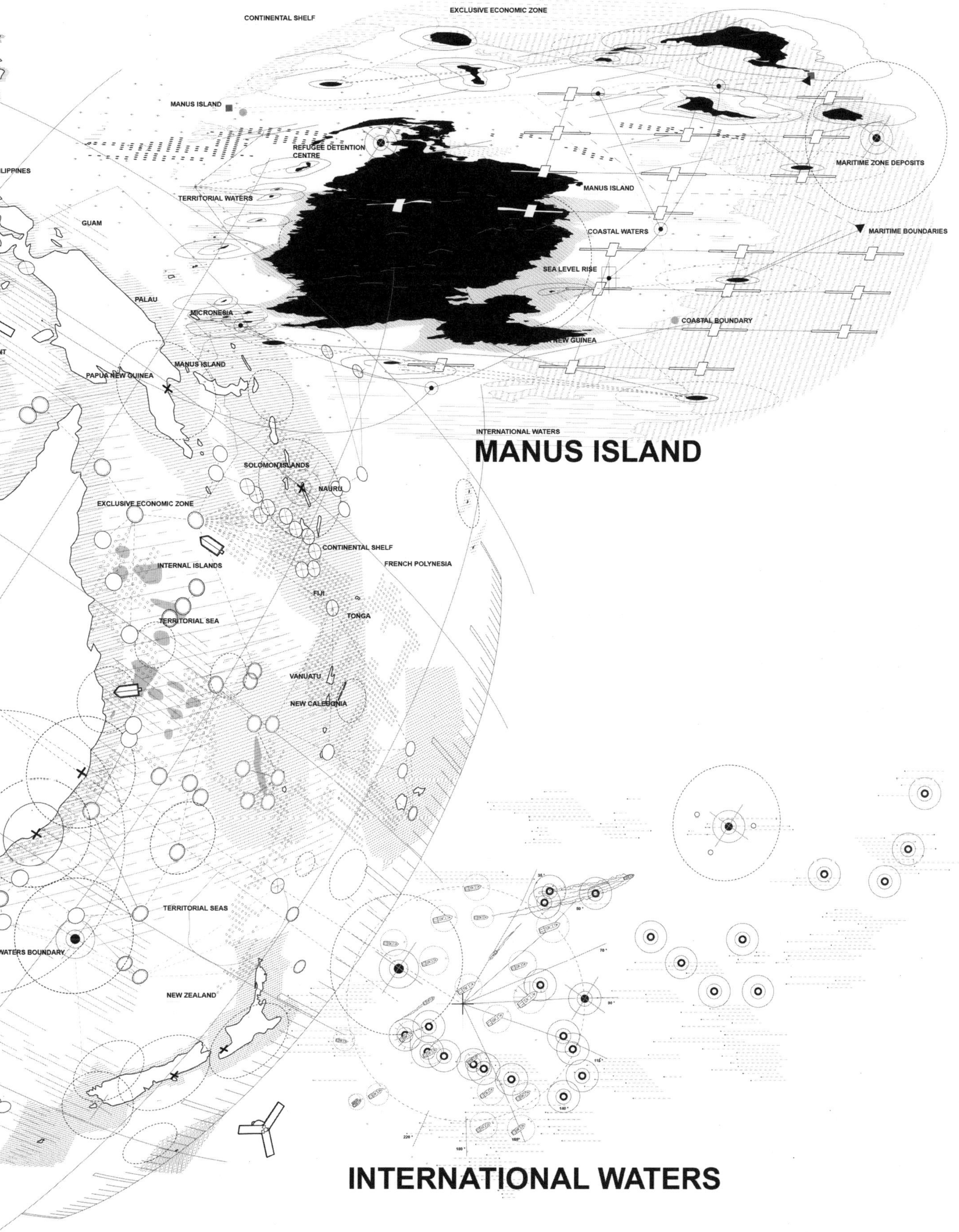
CONTINENTAL SHELF
EXCLUSIVE ECONOMIC ZONE
MANUS ISLAND
REFUGEE DETENTION CENTRE
PHILIPPINES
TERRITORIAL WATERS
MANUS ISLAND
MARITIME ZONE DEPOSITS
GUAM
COASTAL WATERS
MARITIME BOUNDARIES
SEA LEVEL RISE
PALAU
MICRONESIA
COASTAL BOUNDARY
NEW GUINEA
MANUS ISLAND
PAPUA NEW GUINEA
INTERNATIONAL WATERS
MANUS ISLAND
SOLOMON ISLANDS
NAURU
EXCLUSIVE ECONOMIC ZONE
CONTINENTAL SHELF
FRENCH POLYNESIA
INTERNAL ISLANDS
FIJI
TONGA
TERRITORIAL SEA
VANUATU
NEW CALEDONIA
TERRITORIAL SEAS
NEW ZEALAND
INTERNATIONAL WATERS

KHVAY SAMNANG

RUBBER MAN

Words by
Erin Gleeson

Khvay Samnang's Rubber Man confronts a contested landscape with poetic resistance. He responds to the colonial legacy of land use and its effects on Cambodia's indigenous forests and culture today.

The Khmer language transliterates the French transliteration, caoutchouc, of an indigenous South American word for rubber. French Indochina privatised the Khmer monarchy's land in 1884, importing an economic equation that began the physical, conceptual, and spiritual transformation of Cambodia's nature into exploitable land. Hevea seeds were imported from Brazil, and Cambodia's first land concession was established in 1922 for a rubber plantation, which, until 1975, was the largest in the world. Subsequent plantations were concentrated in the highlands, areas home to ancient forests and diverse indigenous populations.

Between 2013 and 2014, Khvay repeatedly travelled to Ratanakiri, Cambodia's north-eastern highland province, an area increasingly known in local and international news for land grabs and protests. The forces behind today's plantations – from individuals to governments to multinationals and international banks – pose a critical threat to indigenous spiritual and agricultural inheritance, which centre on resident forest and ancestor spirits in an elaborate subsistence cycle of planting, transplanting, harvesting, and regeneration – practices that have effectively ensured forest and wildlife conservation for centuries.

Khvay's video installation, Rubber Man, presents this charged landscape, from a remaining village to a clearing, from saplings to mature plantations. The artist takes centre stage, pouring fresh liquid rubber over his body, appearing and disappearing. He wanders through the rational cash crop lines, as if a lost spectre. As the ancient forests are lost, Khvay asks, 'where will the spirits live?'

Rubber Man,
Khvay Samnang, 2014.

Ajna
Babahmetovic

:

SANS SOUCI:
FOUR FACES OF OMARSKA

The Four Faces of Omarska, an ongoing art project conceived by the artist Milica Tomic, evolved from the narrative of a small mine complex called Omarska in Bosnia. The 'four faces' position the mine throughout history. During the socialist era, Omarska mining complex was what its name suggests: a surface iron ore mine. In 1992 during the Bosnian war, Omarska mining complex was turned into a concentration camp; a place of numerous killings and torture. Today, Omarska iron is again being extracted under the control of the transnational steel corporation, ArcelorMittal.
The fourth face of Omarska can be interpreted as the backdrop for the historical film, St George Shoots the Dragon.[1] There is still no memorial for Omarska.

Bosnia today consists of three constitutional nationalities and three entities. (The introduction of the three entities was a direct outcome of the war.) The resulting government has three presidents, and a clear territorial and ethnic division within the country that keeps Bosnia in a constant state of limbo. Hence the ignorance and inconceivable negligence of a proper commemoration for Omarska and it's history becomes conceivable.

The studio Sans Souci: Four Faces of Omarska was conducted by Milica Tomic in 2016 at the Institute of the Contemporary Art at Graz University of Technology. Students were invited to investigate and learn about the post-conflict urban and social structures in Bosnia today.

The concentration camps Omarska and Trnopolje have been the focus of the studio as unexplored, not memorialised spaces of conflict during the war in Bosnia in the 1990s. The architecture and forms of the former camps are deeply intertwined with the present state of affairs and heavily affect the urban and social structures today. Landscapes containing mass graves and undiscovered remains have been exploited and neglected. This maintains an ongoing state of conflict thus furthering firm territorial, social and economic divisions within the country.

Political agendas and globalisation transform architecture and landscapes into conflicting spaces, polluting them to the extent that their initial (or present) value can hardly be recognised. Purification of these spaces is unimaginable in the permanent state of war. Students produced an exhibition in which all of the collected knowledge was presented in the form of videos, photos, writings, interviews and an opening performance. This exhibition created an entry point to the knowledge gathered; the objective was to present a tool for understanding the inception and course of such disruptive practices in order to understand the state we are in today .

1. 'Sveti Georgije ubiva aždahu (St George Shoots the Dragon)', 2007, motion picture, Sinears Wild Bunch, Serbia, directed by Srdjan Dragojevic.

Sans Souci: Four Faces of Omarska exhibition
Image credit: Dzana Ajanovic

J10-M-808

One of the numerous 'Temples of Sadness and Loneliness' as Sudbin, prisoner of the camp Trnopolje, calls them. Those houses are those of the diaspora, people who fled war and visit Bosnia occasionally. They still dream of coming back and build huge, perfectly trimmed houses as a symbol of hope, sadness but also defiance. 'The ones without the facade are surely from some returnees', continues Sudbin.
Image credit: Therese Eberl

Above:
Former Trnopolje camp, now school.
Image credit: Ina Lichtenegger

Right:
Survivors of the camp next to the memorial of a mass grave.
Image credit: Simon Oberhofer

Sans Souci: Four Faces of Omarska exhibition.
Image credit: Dzana Ajanovic

Sans Souci: Four Faces of Omarska is a Master Project conducted by the Institute for Contemporary Art at the Graz University of Technology Exhibition. This project included interviews with Sudbin Music, Satko Mujagic, Berina Ramic, Milorad Kremenovic, and Namka Konjevic.

The project was run by Milica Tomic, Simon Oberhofer, Lidija K. Radojevic, Dubravka Sekulic, and Dr. Daniel Gethmann.

Guest lecturers: Srdan Hercigonja , Dr. Andrew Herscher, Satko Mujagic, Sudbin Music

Participating students: Amina Abazovic, Džana Ajanovic, Ajna Babahmetovic, Therese Eberl, Helena Katharina Eichlinger, Angelika Hinterbrandner, Muris Kalic, Aldin Kanuric, Anousheh Kehar, Amir Ihab Tharwat Kozman, Ina Barbara Lichtenegger, Hilette Lindeque, Melissa Muhri, Alisa Pekic, Tina Petek, Andrea Pekovic, Clara Primschitz and Philipp Sattler.

Kasia Keeley & Andrew Prindle

:

INTERACTING WITH OUR NUCLEAR LANDSCAPES

[A]rt suggests a way for us to see the world in which we live, and, by seeing it, to accept it and integrate it into our sensibility. The open work assumes the task of giving us an image of discontinuity. It does not narrate it; it is it. It takes on a mediating role between the abstract categories of science and the living matter of our sensibility; it almost becomes a sort of transcendental scheme that allows us to comprehend new aspects of the world.
Umberto Eco[1]

There are three rest stops along US Route 24 containing information about the surrounding environment. On a clear day, the Columbia River's last undammed section can be seen moving past Hanford's entombed reactors – material relics from the site's former plutonium production.[2] The Hanford Reach National Monument has placed signs at each rest stop describing the site's transformations: from ancient geology and Native American territory, to its use by the Department of Energy (DOE), to a preserved and protected shrub steppe ecosystem. However, none of these signs make mention of the ongoing clean-up consolidating structures, equipment, soil, and contaminated sludge into the Environmental Restoration Disposal Facility (ERDF).

For over forty-four years, Hanford's 586 square miles were a military nuclear production ground and the landscape was widely treated as waste disposal for irradiated by-products resulting from operations. In response to Hanford's 1988 designation as a Superfund site, the DOE began creating ERDF in an attempt to contain the dispersed pollutants and prevent further environmental degradation. However, there is a nearly invisible persistent movement of irradiated material through the soil, air and water of the landscape. While the clean-up effort works to diminish outflow of these materials from the site, it is an impossible task. Tumbleweed is but one example. The invasive plant's roots can descend great distances – potentially extracting toxic groundwater – and then go wherever the wind blows them.[3] While some are caught by the barbed fencing, others eschew the DOE's territorial boundary. The pervasive diffusion of irradiated materials prevents a complete elimination of waste, making the DOE's clean-up effort more of a strategic material reorganisation than a return of the landscape to pre-Hanford conditions.

The environmental consequences of Hanford's production during the Manhattan Project and the Cold War created a wicked ecology that is not readily legible to passers-by. Physical distancing from the material evidence of the site's former use and present operations disengages people from the ongoing impact of Hanford. The DOE and National Park Service (NPS) have set up tours to the B Reactor – the first reactor to go online and a National Historic Landmark – and ERDF. However, each tour presents curated narratives celebrating technological ingenuity and excellence, leaving little room for the complex waste legacy unfolding in the landscape.

While the amount of waste that has accrued over forty-four years of operation may be spatially incomprehensible, there is indeed a size and scale to ERDF. The disposal cells at ERDF are 400 feet wide, 1000 feet long, 60 feet deep and will rise 20 feet above the landscape once capped. These cells currently occupy 107 acres with new cells added to accommodate the DOE's clean-up effort as needed. Akin to standing next to a strip mine, ERDF represents an industrial solution to a military-industrial problem.

Our design proposes two installations to engage ERDF through methods not employed by the DOE. Site I and Site II each replicate the dimensions of a single ERDF cell and place it across roads running along Hanford's boundaries. Half of each site will excavate 60 feet down, and the other half will use excavated soil to lift the topography 20 feet above grade with a concrete wall bisecting the cut/fill operation. Visitors to Site I descend to the bottom of the wall and at Site II they may walk to the top. Embedded within the concrete wall at each site is a glass chamber devoid of anything, including waste. Site I is oriented towards the Democratic Republic of the Congo, where significant portions of uranium were mined for weapons; Site II points to Nagasaki, Japan, where Hanford's plutonium was used to end World War II. Through these orientations, each site connects visitors to global sites of extraction and deposition that have resulted in destruction far greater than what is immediately visible.

1. Eco, U 1989, The Open Work, translated by A Cancogni, Cambridge, MA: Harvard University Press: Cambridge, p. 90.

2. Blaine, H 1996, A River Lost: The Life and Death of the Columbia, W.W. Norton & Company New York, p. 148.

3. Cram, S 2015, 'Wild and scenic wasteland: Conservation politics in the nuclear wilderness', Environmental Humanities, vol 7, pp. 89-105.

4. Alvarez, R 2017, 'West Lake story: An underground fire, radioactive waste, and governmental failure', Bulletin of the Atomic Scientists, <http://thebulletin.org/west-lake-story-underground-fire-radioactive-waste-and-governmental-failure9160>.

Site 1,
Three years after installation.
Image credit: Keeley & Prindle

Site 2,
First year of installation.
Image credit: Keeley & Prindle

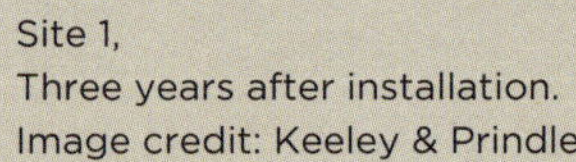

Site 1,
Three years after installation.
Image credit: Keeley & Prindle

Hanford tank farm.
Image credit: Keeley & Prindle

The installations are not meant to be flashy tourist attractions with kiosks, parking or simplistic signage. There is no attempted re-naturalisation of the landscape. Instead, greater disturbance provokes questions: Why is this here? Where am I looking? Only information that locally and globally situates a person is included, and it is up to the visitor to independently seek out the site's history. In this way, the design rejects tools typically employed at monuments that control narratives and feign comprehension. Rather, the installations provide visitors with the opportunity to personally situate themselves between past and present, the far away and the immediate.

These installations use the tools of industry to comment on industry. Influenced by the land art movement, this work does not try to ameliorate or diminish the impact Hanford has on the surrounding environment. Instead, it uses ERDF's dimensions as a scalar tool to better connect the visitor with key parts of our nuclear heritage too often overlooked: nuclear violence and waste legacies. Fixed solutions or narratives are not presented, and the installations disrupt the landscape to demonstrate the scale of one ongoing attempt at containing waste. The displacement of soil, division by concrete walls, and hollow glass columns each speak to the consequences of moving vast amounts of material and people for nuclear armament.

The pervasive pollution at Hanford, while exceptional, is not unique. The ongoing consequences of nuclear weapons and waste will continue to impact the world in ways that cannot be ameliorated or erased. Design should engage the public with landscapes of waste as a way to reveal the unconfined impacts of reconfiguring landscapes to produce power through territory and narrative. These proposed interventions do not focus on the scientific and engineering accomplishments of Hanford essential to the heritage discourse of the DOE and NPS, but on the exploitive, extractive, and environmentally degrading military-industrial operation that has created a legacy within the landscape that will last for hundreds of thousands of years.

Hotham Street Ladies

AUTUMN MOON OVER POTATO BLOSSOM MOUNTAIN

In an increasingly globalised world where traditional food cultures are rapidly giving way to Western fast food, The Hotham Street Ladies present Autumn Moon over Potato Blossom Mountain.

Inspired by a 2013 image of South Korean teenagers throwing a 'potato party' in response to a McDonalds french fry discount, Autumn Moon over Potato Blossom Mountain references the excessive consumption inherent in the images of french fries piled across the table. Does this scene represent our failing food culture or provide motivation for change and preservation of food diversity?

The mountain landscape of icing, fries, sauce, nuggets and burgers - replete with a ketchup waterfall - in the installation juxtaposes this contemporary food phenomenon with the traditional Korean 'true-view' landscape painting movement, in which Korean artists broke from Chinese traditions to focus on their own cultural identity and depiction of the Korean environment.

Autumn Moon over Potato Blossom Mountain provokes us to explore the humble potato and its capacity to feed us into the future.

Whether or not climate change will adversely affect the potato growing industry is controversial. Some scientists predict a devastating effect on this important crop, which is a dietary staple of many cultures, therefore bringing into focus the possibility of increased poverty and starvation in some parts of the world. Will Autumn Moon over Potato Blossom Mountain become a scene within a museum documenting a food stock deeply rooted in the culture of a bygone era?

Equally, other scientists are predicting that potatoes will still be grown in some regions of the world and might turn out to be more robust than other vegetables. In this case potatoes could make up an even greater proportion of the diet in many parts of the world. Will Autumn Moon over Potato Blossom Mountain appear less gluttonous, and more a normal portrayal of everyday life in the future?

Autumn Moon over Potato Blossom Mountain was an exhibition as part Absolutely Famished, a creative exploration of future food and the twenty-second century marketplace curated by Dr Renee Beale at University of Melbourne's Carlton Connect Initiative.

Autumn Moon over
Potato Blossom Mountain, 2016,
Icing fondant, royal icing, icing
sugar and food dye.
Image credit: Hotham Street Ladies

WE DREAM OF NETWORKS

DISRUPTIVE
DISRUPTIVE
DISRUPTIVE
DISRUPTIVE
DISRUPTIVE
DISRUPTIVE
DISRUPTIVE
DISRUPTIVE
DISRUPTIVE
DISRUPTIVE
DISRUPTIVE
DISRUPTIVE
DISRUPTIVE
DISRUPTIVE

Julian Day

:

COMMON SOUND: HOW CAN SOUND HELP US UNDERSTAND THE POLITICS OF PUBLIC SPACE?

Any landscape, whether street, mall, railway station or park, is an intersection of competing energies. A person avoids a speeding car. A tree bows to the wind. Two dogs bark at each other. Every action implicates the others, creating an ever-shifting vibrational matrix. We can map this geography by listening to its sounds and analysing how they interact. This can help us view, or indeed hear, a landscape as a system of interlocking power relations. Sounds reflect degrees of intention and privilege. Is one sound louder than another? Does one spread further? If a sound enters another's domain is it welcomed? How do two sounds meet and what does this reveal about the relationship between the sources?

Sound can reveal what the eye cannot see. Typically, sound spreads freely through space, an itinerant movement that transcends the partitions that we use to corral different energies, such as walls and other barriers. Being invisible, sound does so by stealth. Observing where a sound goes can illuminate the hidden rules and boundaries of a location, its unseen socio-political paths. A useful concept here is the 'acoustic arena'. The sonic-spatial theorists Barry Blesser and Linda-Ruth Salter define this as 'the experience of a social spatiality, where the listener is connected to the sound-producing activities of other individuals'.[1] We can extrapolate this concept to view acoustic arenas as comprising various personal spaces that can overlap, abut and clash. Their intermingling reveals much about how the actors within a space operate.

This idea drives Super Critical Mass, a participatory sound project that uses dispersed homogeneous sound to investigate how people co-experience common environments. It brings together 'temporary communities' who perform communal sonic actions in various locations using multiple mobile identical sound sources, whether musical (flutes, harmonicas, voice), everyday objects (plates, coins, pieces of wood) or even the infrastructure of a place (iron girders, tables, floors). The structure of each work evolves from the participants' interactions with each other and with their immediate environment. This creates a dynamic feedback situation, a co-dependent mingling of acoustic arenas, that I call 'interdependent listening'.

Super Critical Mass has worked in many types of public space including parks, libraries, galleries, streets and malls. Each location has an existing sonic profile that Super Critical Mass counterpoints with a contrasting uniformity created by the dispersed identical sounds. Introducing this sound field brings existing relationships into clearer perspective while complicating the aural depth of field of both performers and listeners. Thus, depending on the specific actions, the works are subtly or overtly disruptive.

A recent example was Games And Actions (for a Quiet City), presented for the City of Sydney in 2015. The work comprised three performances in three locations, each with a specific sonic profile: an undulating rainforest of handbells in Hyde Park; discreet fields of white noise generated by coins on table tops in the neo-classical Mitchell Library; and the interplay between ceramic bowls dragged by the feet across slate, blurring with passing traffic in the semi-covered thoroughfare of Martin Place.

1. Blesser, B & Salter, L 2009, Spaces Speak, Are You Listening?: Experiencing Aural Architecture, The MIT Press, Cambridge, p.25.

Gean Moreno &
Ernesto Oroza

:

NOTES ON THE TABLOID PROJECT: MODELS OF DISPERSAL

Manif d'Art 5, Quebec City Biennial, 2010. This tabloid was inserted in the local weekly VOIR, which is distributed through the city. Decorative modules were pasted in certain locations throughout the city as 'placeholder'/ 'signal' of the distributive project.

Image credit: Moreno & Oroza

Some old women use newspaper to dye their grey hair. They rub the pages insistently on strands of hair until the ink dust released seeps all the way down to their follicles. Afterward, the new blackness, so deeply entrenched at first, slowly abandons their heads and stains the pillowcases. In the washer, these pillowcases stain the rest of the clothes that they're spinning with. A dark colour starts spreading inside the house. Ink that not a week ago had been employed to convey timely information, is reconfigured as vague spots on the grandchildren's uniform shirts and as a new shade on the son's once-white work pullovers. But the inked water, as this is happening, has already left the domestic space behind. Through the foam expelled by the washer, and running down the different drainage systems, it expands infinitely. A river of inked water roars through the plumbing, and eventually escapes through corroded pipes, faulty unions and cracked elbows, and invades the city.

Each washer is just a single source of this inked water, but there are thousands of them in the city. Imagine them synchronised, erupting simultaneously from the penthouses on Brickell Avenue, from the backyards in Hialeah and the hospitals in Allapattah, from the women's prison on Krome Avenue, from the shotgun houses in Overtown and the pseudo-Moroccan single-family homes in Opa-locka and from kitchens in Little Havana duplexes. Suddenly, there would be innumerable tributaries, feeding on one another. The entire city, in this situation, is recast as a tidal basin. Currents would constantly gain strength. Eventually, they overflow onto the streets and other existing axes that channel them. Tributaries merge. The inked water and the foam begin to slip under doors, seep through the crevices in solid walls, run off into sewers and canals until these too overflow and so it continues.

Puddles remain in the wake of the foam and impure liquid. Their waters fill the grooves in truck tyres and are pulled all the way to the port and onto ships running cargo across the sea. They also splash when messengers and food delivery folks race over them with their bikes and scooters. The packages they are carrying are soaked. This is how the inked water climbs through the hollow shaft of the elevator into office towers and stains the curtains in the conference rooms, the carpet, the linoleum tiles in the break rooms.

As the puddles grow shallow, dispersed, the wet asphalt still manages to blacken the soles of students' shoes as they, wearing shirts their grandmothers stained in the wash, cut across empty lots and fenced properties, carving new paths through the city in order to get to schools and vocational centres on time and avoid afternoon detentions.

As the water finally evaporates completely, it leaves behind an ink residue, a black powder like the one that some old ladies tease out of newspapers to dye their grey hair. This black powder, the routes it marks, draws a new map of the city. These currents of inked water are real, of course; they spread across the memories and imaginations of any child who has seen grandma dye her hair with newspaper, who has seen the smudgy stains on her pillowcase, the stains on their own uniforms. But they are also virtual. These are currents that mark a physical passage as much as they mark the movement of a series of habits, of traditions, of vernacular and familial practices, of knowledge that has been handed down from one generation to another, taken from one geographical context to another. They are channels of information. Just as the lines marking the large systems of distribution that tabloids employ are also channels of this sort. These, too, are real; they're there, even if they have no continuous physical manifestation. They are one of the city's invisible materialities, a virtual channel for one of its flows. They are plotted only by the spots where users pick up their tabloids, by the habits that drive these users to go every week to the same place, expecting new stories but always within a series of specific and familiar graphic parameters. These systems of distribution draw a new city over the grid that we find on dusty maps and diagrams employed in architecture and urbanism schools.

Employing a standardised typology, our tabloids slip into systems of production and distribution in which this typology is a central component. Or rather, they emerge as a kind of altered offspring, a teratological experiment from these systems. For a project in Quebec City last spring, for instance, our tabloid was inserted (dissolved) in the city's free weekly, VOIR. It existed in a run of 15,000 copies, spread through a series of delivery routes that covered a significant portion of the city. Our tabloid, no longer an autonomous artefact but grafted like a parasite to a temporary host, exploited a massive system of efficient distribution which, on the one hand, dispersed it throughout the city and, on the other, tapped into habitual behaviours of the local population to further enlarge the territory through which the tabloid travelled.

But, as a parasite, the tabloid may burrow deeper than these distributive systems. It may tunnel down into the substructures of the standard tabloid, into the very codes that organise it as both a cultural/social artefact or sign, and a unit within a productive system.

The newspaper printer is, above all, a distributor of multiples or identicals, similar to a machine for injecting plastic or one for stamping metal. Reconsidering such a system in its pre-cultural moment, that is, suspended before the usual social function of its product has been enabled, allows us to insert an altered product with an altered social function. With this alteration, the system multiplies an object that is different from the one it usually produces. But the multiplicative and serial mode of production is essential here. Its logic cannot avoid marking the parasitical 'material.' Knowing this, one has to consider how this multiplicative or serial element may be employed fruitfully. One works with it. And what products can better exploit processes of multiplication than those with the capacity to organise themselves modularly, in potentially infinite spreads; objects that can couple into larger continuums that themselves become new and different objects? A modular pattern printed on a tabloid page is pregnant with inexhaustible potential. The pattern favours and can participate in the configuration of a plane or a structure. It compels all the identical units spat out by the printing press to produce a condition emergent in the relationship between them that is greater than the individual object and that exists at a distance from the individual object's usual moment and form of consumption.

Methodologically, the project may deal less with the alteration of a generic product than with a 'genetic' intervention in its productive substrate, with planting an invasive cultural sign in the optimised space of generic production. With an awareness of the qualities this invasive species is prone to, due to the very nature of the system it has taken as host; it, too, like any generic object, will be optimised to the point of abstraction, to where it takes on the condition of something inevitable in the city, like linoleum tiles, drop ceiling tiles and sheetrock panels.

In Quebec City, we employed a schematic version of a vernacular decorative pattern that we found on the facade of a house in Little Haiti, a spread of banal faux stones. A question quickly emerged: how can this pattern overcome its suspicious quality as a parasite? How does it slip into a kind of normality, of 'genericity'? It has to exploit ambiguity, reappropriate familiar codes. The insertion of a foreign sign (say, the reproduction of false stones) needs to be associated with a text or some other common element in the language of the newspaper. It needs to activate other functions, be they indicative, illustrative, commercial, or documentary.
The pattern, as foreign or intrusive element, remains exceptional but within a very familiar and schematic structure. It can't obviate the defining qualities of the typology it has invaded. One imagines that a tabloid that is all patterns or that is highly idiosyncratic in some other way always risks becoming the sort of graphic project that is produced for the protected space of galleries and museums; its meaning and autonomy upheld at the expense of the social function and mobility of the typology it appropriates. Something vital, the way the tabloid moves through the city, simultaneously unseen and ubiquitous, organically woven into the urban flows, would be irrevocably lost from such an iteration of the tabloid. Its condition as a vector of information, as a familiar structure, as a natural inhabitant of an urban ecology, as an artefact that is embedded within the larger economic forces of the city, in short, all that is interesting about the tabloid, would be smeared out of the picture or diluted to a sad and unimportant state.

In the text that accompanied the pattern inserted in the Quebec City weekly, which sought to mimic (in structure, if not in content) any run-of- the-mill tabloid article with its geometry of columns and requisite accompanying photos, we spoke of a running surface of plywood sheets that was covering certain sections of Miami in the wake of

Manif d'Art 5, Quebec City Biennial, 2010. This tabloid was inserted in the local weekly VOIR, which is distributed through the city. Decorative modules were pasted in certain locations throughout the city as 'placeholder'/ 'signal' of the distributive project.
Image credit: Moreno & Oroza

a massive wave of home foreclosures. Banks seal empty houses with plywood sheets over the doors and windows to keep squatters, junkies and thieves out. Many people in Quebec associated, strangely to our ears, the rock pattern produced by Haitian immigrants (as a microscopic version) with the multiplying plywood plane. One, the rock pattern, we thought, was an effort to claim at the level of the home and the family, by deploying a decorative structure, space for a particular value system. The other, the plywood sheets, we thought as potentially endless urban wallpaper that spoke of the massive force of an economic crisis. In fact, we propose in the text that the knots and the grains of the plywood added up to the repeating 'decorative' pattern of a catastrophe that no one could figure out how to avert. The goal in bringing these two very different patterns (and worlds) together was to highlight different patterns of expansion that, in their forceful multiplication, in the ineluctable character that their growth assumed, served as metaphors for the way we imagined our tabloid, and tabloids in general, spreading through the city.

There is a virtual or abstract plane, after all, on which the 15,000 modules distributed in Quebec City can be collected. On it, they produce an enormous alien surface that threatens to blanket the entire city. Like the snow that covers its streets every winter, but climbs the city's vertical surfaces instead, there is also a map, perhaps not yet drawn but real all the same, of the truck routes through which VOIR is delivered. There is a potential drawing that documents the distribution points where the stacks of weeklies are dropped off. It would be made up of the doorways and stoops in front of bars, record shops, bookstores, corner stores, cafes, fast food restaurants, cultural institutions and student centres. Maybe it's just a set of coordinates or address numbers. Each of the metal stands and bins in which VOIR is kept, in turn, is a node in yet another possible sketch of tangled trajectories.

There is, finally, an imaginable theoretical plane, a narrative space, on which the final consumption and use of the pattern can be documented. One imagines the Little Haiti rocks, having migrated further north, used as wallpaper in a record store, in a dorm, in the bathroom of a bar; or used as a doily or as a book cover, as a picture frame. The pattern can be used to wrap beer bottles outside the bodegas where it is illegal to loiter and drink. It can be employed to cover and replace dislikeable or out-dated posters, to run over bare city walls, and to wrap around telephone poles lined with unpalatable concert flyers and party announcements. It can be used as a decorative layer over the glass of all the empty storefronts in a faltering mall. It would certainly brighten the mood of the place. It can cover the plywood sheets that seal homes that have been foreclosed or the rotting wooden fences around abandoned construction sites. It can be used by some old ladies to dye their grey hair.

Once the information vectors of Quebec City were contaminated, the expansion of the Little Haiti rock pattern threatened to be endless, to dissolve into the city.

Hayden Matthys

:

APPROACHING [NON]SITE IN THE POSTHUMAN

Traditionally in landscape architecture, site has been approached as a mark of separation between the human and their environment; a way of bounding or framing space in order to define a limit within which to approach it.[1] This framing implies a way of looking at site through a constant unit of measure, and for some four hundred years 'since the Renaissance' this unit of measure has been the human body.[2] Because of this, site has always been expandable or reducible to a human understanding of space. The problem with this understanding of site is that it is based in a world of modernism in which we no longer find ourselves.[3]

Approaching [Non]Site in the Posthuman is an enquiry into the contemporary site in landscape architecture. Born from a need to question the traditional authority of the human derived scale for site - at a time when the rate of change in our current epoch has moved beyond our human comprehension - this project argues for a rethinking of our role as landscape architects in a posthuman landscape.[4] Posthuman theory, following the work of Rosi Braidotti, has been selected to engender a shifting of the system of thought through which site is approached, an opportunity to 'devise new social, ethical and discursive schemes of subject formation to match the profound transformations we are undergoing'.[5] These 'profound transformations' refer to a question for our species of how to live in the wake of new ethical and political challenges, at a time of increased global connectivity and environmental commodification in a capitalist system hell-bent on consumption.[6] Here the idea of 'post-anthropocentrism' is key to posthuman theory, as it is a call for a rethinking of the relationship between human and materials within this global system.[7] Employing a new-materialist methodology to rethink the formation of site - reducing all elements that make site to the same unit of measure - site will be unpacked through 'the material agency or effectivity of non-human or not-quite- human things'.[8] I am making a link between posthumanism and new-materialist theory here as a way of critiquing the current scale of site representation and engagement in contemporary landscape practice. Leading to an investigation and subsequent discussion of site as matter, palimpsest, and process. A move, as the title suggests, towards an understanding of site not as a space but as a '...spacing which is the condition for everything to take place, for everything to be inscribed'.[9] A Smithsonian non-site, a space of in-betweenness and 'becoming': site in a constant state of being made.[10] There is a link to be made between metaphor and representation on this point of the non-site, due to its ties with narrative and land art, which positions the project as a questioning of the edge or boundary of site. This questioning of site shall be grounded in the coastal town of Narrawong in Western Victoria, where, through a new-materialist lens, the basic unit of measure for our species shall be critiqued through a reframing of the role of the human in the posthuman landscape. Here the act of material displacement - both as a physical description of moving matter and a displacement of the conventional hierarchy of material - becomes a metaphor for the entire project. An interaction with site as process, and an engagement with site as narrative, toward an understanding of site beyond that of the human.

The death of the contemporary site

The vast utopian ideals of order and control, of form following function, have been replaced by a '...spatial life today [that] is as much immaterial as it is physical, as much bound into time and relational connections as it is to traditional notions of enclosure and "place"'.[11] Site has undergone a spatial mutation in this sense, yet there has been no mutation of the human able to keep up with this new site operating at scales beyond our comprehension. In this new posthuman world 'architecture can no longer be bound by the static conditions of space and place, here and there. In a mediated world, there are no longer places in the sense that we used to know them'.[12] It is just this rigidity of viewing that new-materialism allows us to address for a move towards a posthuman understanding of site. In this world of materials there is no disjunction between objects, all are connected and interrelated through being viewed at the same unit of measure (matter). In this way there is an overlap between the human and the non-human, or as Ingold says '...in the world of materials, humans figure as much within the context for stone as do stones within the context for humans. And these contexts, far from lying on disparate levels of being, respectively social and natural, are established as overlapping regions of

1. Eisenman, P 2007, Written Into the Void: Selected Writings, 1990-2004, Yale University Press, New Haven, Conn.

2. Kipnis, J & Leeser, T (eds) 1997, Chora L Works: Jacques Derrida and Peter Eisenman, Monacelli Press, New York.

3. Jameson, F 1991, Postmodernism, or, The Cultural Logic of Late Capitalism (Post-Contemporary Interventions), Duke University Press, Durham.

4. David, H 2016, 'Defining the territories of landscape practice: Towards the Neo infrastructural', Kerb, no. 24, pp. 40-45.

5. Braidotti, R 2013, The Posthuman, Polity Press, Cambridge, UK.

6. Simon, J 2013, Neomaterialism, A. Altman (ed.), Sternberg Press, Berlin.

7. Wolfe, C 2010, What is Posthumanism, University of Minnesota Press, Minneapolis.

8. Ibid 2.

9. Bennett, J 2009, Vibrant Matter A Political Ecology of Things, Duke University Press, North Carolina.

10. Ibid 2.

11. Corner, J 2011, 'The Agency of Mapping: Speculation, Critique and Invention', In M Dodge, R Kitchen, C Perkins (eds.), The Map Reader: Theories of Mapping Practice and Cartographic Representation, John Wiley & Sons, Chichester, UK, pp. 89-101.

12. Ibid 3.

Opposite:
The Spectacle of the Absurd.

the same world'.[13] This is an important position to take for the posthuman, for it challenges the basic unit of measure for our species and confronts the traditional authority of the human as the maker of site. This shake-up of the hierarchy is what is needed in order to confront the position of the human in a posthuman world. It is a break with traditions set up in classical architecture and confirmed in modernism.[14] Opening up the possibilities for an engagement with site in landscape architecture that goes beyond that of a traditional human understanding of space.

The non-site of representation and measure

It is argued by Braidotti that '...the posthuman is fought precisely at the level of representation, symbolism meaning, and thus (among other 'media') in language'.[15] It is interesting for Braidotti to use the very human trait of 'language' here as a part of the battleground for her posthumanism, for isn't the human the topic Braidotti is attempting to rethink? In reading this for my own approach to posthumanism I would say, at this point, that it is about the way language communicates a predetermined meaning for a thing, and thus a rethinking of the meaning of the object is also a rethinking of language. This is the role representation has to play for a posthuman approach to site, a way of describing the world of materials through making their power in the creation of site apparent through their rendering and subsequent reading in space. Corner and Mclean, in their text Taking Measures across the American Landscape, speak on the role of representation and its relationship to a measuring of space.

While it is inevitable that the codes and conventions of measurement are bound into the prevailing ideology and power relations of the time, the land itself is ultimately resistant to human control and objectivist reduction. If the practices of domination and control are indeed futile in the face of nature, then perhaps measure might be deployed in such a way as to privilege doubt, approximation, and propriety over the illusion of absolute certainty.[16]
Expanding on Corner's position that the conventions of measurement are tied to the ideology of power at the time of the measuring, I am arguing for a re-representation of site through a new-materialist lens in order to measure site through materials, as the way of beginning a retraining of the human understanding of site in the posthuman. It is here that the non-site, and its relationship to narrative and symbolism, becomes a powerful tool for questioning site in the posthuman.

There is a line in Albert Camus' The Myth of Sisyphus that opens up this questioning. He says, describing Sisyphus and his stone, that 'Each atom of that stone, each mineral flake of that night filled mountain, in itself forms a world'.[17] Here, Sisyphus' rock (the material) is the non-site. Non-site implies a condition of presence in a condition of absence that, when applied to the narrative of an object removed from its context (what I am calling the displaced material) asks questions around the limit and scale of site.[18]

Between the non-site of the displaced material and the actual site of the context, sits the space of significance for this new understanding of site in landscape architecture. It is in this space that this questioning of the limit and scale of site occurs. The displaced material opens up questions surrounding site that follows the view of Peter Eisenman and Jacques Derrida in their project for a garden in Tschumi's Park de la Villette titled Chora L Works.

They say, talking of moving stones, that: 'The object is formed by the receptacle and the traces of the receptacle are left on the object. At the same time, the object forms the receptacle and leaves traces on it. It is a reverberating, displacing activity'.[19] This questioning comes from the displaced material still retaining a meaning of its own even when devoid of the context in which it was formed. A non-site as it is representative of the context in which it was formed and also, as Camus says, 'in itself forms a world'.[20]

Therefore site is reducible to a single material, or able to be reduced even further to the interaction between matter. It is through this shifting of the measure (the scale of viewing) that site in the posthuman becomes a constantly expanding and shrinking phenomena. A non-site that opens up site as both a physical space and a narrative, of which neither is more important or more real than the other.

Paludal:
Clay

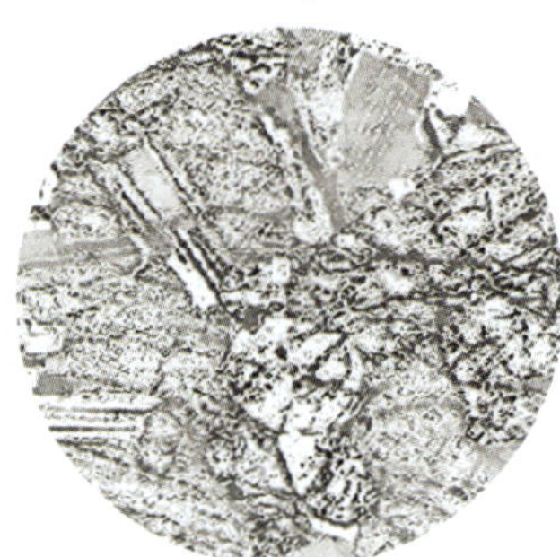

Extrusive:
Basalt

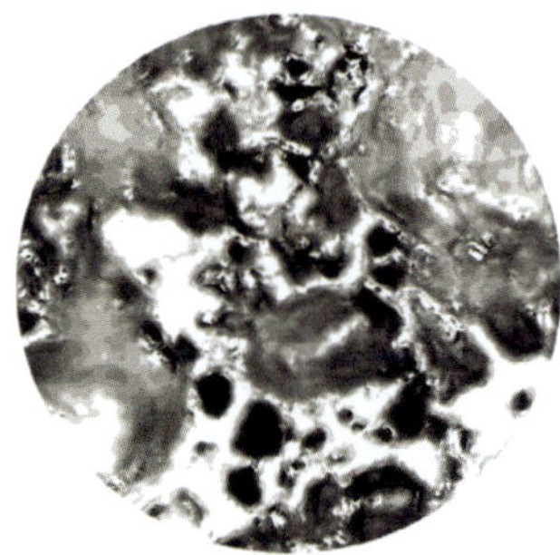

Paludal:
Silt

Aeolian:
Sand

At the end of his long effort measured by skyless space and time without depth, the purpose is achieved. Then Sisyphus watches the stone rush back down in a few moments toward that lower world whence he will have to push it up again toward the summit. He goes back down to the plain.[21]

There is another interesting comparison to be drawn between this project and Camus' The Myth of Sisyphus, which follows on from Braidotti's position that the posthuman is fought at the level of symbolism. In the same way that Camus uses Sisyphus and his task of pushing a rock uphill, only to watch it roll back down, as a metaphor for the futility of the human in the face of the absurdity of existence; so too does this project use the action of the displaced material to reflect the role of humanity in the posthuman. The idea of the myth has grown alongside the idea of the non-site in this project. I am using the term myth here because of its relationship to symbolism in its storytelling. Symbolism becomes important for this project, as the project is a retraining of the perception of site through an immersing of the human in a narrative of new-materialist site formation. Materials, under this methodology of new-materialism, are regarded as the objects through which site is built, and the symbols through which a posthuman understanding of site is communicated.

The space that shall act as the testing ground for this is the coastal town of Narrawong in Western Victoria, in particular the relationship between Mt Clay (a low rising mountain that occupies the northern aspect of the town) and the river mouth of the Surry (that marks the southern edge).

Narrawong as a site - in the traditional use of the word - is in a constant state of change. The river mouth and banks of the Surry are constantly shifting in relation to periods of high rainfall, with the river only meeting the Southern Ocean in the midst of winter.[22] This has led to a contest between the river edge and the encroaching farmland, with the human occupants of Narrawong electing to fight against this system of flux through engineered solutions, whether that be a static seawall or the illegal opening of the river mouth; a physical manifestation of the hierarchy of the human, built from a contemporary view of site.[23]

The chosen design move intended to question this hierarchy of the human, is that of material displacement, following the discussion around the non-site in the previous section. An engagement with materials as symbols is a move against their commodification in contemporary practice, a rethinking of the role of materials born from a rethinking of the scale at which site is viewed.[24]
Through site-as-matter, if we apply classical mechanics as a metaphor here, we can say that materiality would be the minerals that make the stone - its texture, colour, and so on. But materialism is the force of gravity, the force that makes the stone, determining its relations with other things...we can now regard materialism as being also the gravity within the stone. The scheme alters the stone itself.[25]

In new-materialism the process of formation becomes more important than the outcome, for in the world of materials any outcome for site is only a momentary snapshot of a space at a particular point in time. Because of this, site in the posthuman lends itself to a reading of site as a palimpsest, a way of looking aligned to Eisenman's reading of Proust where site encompasses all that it has been in its present moment of existence.[24] Therefore site is not viewed as a surface, but rather as a receptacle of unfolding processes, and if we engage with site in this way, it allows for a design project that acts across time scales that transcend that of the human. Removing the traditional authority of site as a human construct through a deconstruction of the human as the measure of space.[25] For in the scope of site-as- matter, the human is simply one part in the processes of site. This deconstruction fundamentally shifts site from an immediate experience to one of change, calling for a reading of site across generations, a measuring of site more aligned to the geologic than the human. This understanding of site as process is simultaneous an understanding of site as a constant reading and writing of space. In this sense, each material that makes site is understood in terms of a spatial narrative. A story continuously being written by the interplay of matter, which is both constantly forming and being formed by site.[26] The narrative is important here as it gives hierarchy to materials that, in the anthropocentric view, would be regarded as being of lesser value than the human in the making of site.

13. Ingold, T 2011, Being Alive Essays on Movement, Knowledge and Description, Taylor and Francis, Hoboken.

14. Ibid 2.

15. Herbrechter, S & Braidotti, R 2013, 'The Posthuman, "Culture Machine"', <http://www.culturemachine.net/index.php/cm/article/view/495/516>.

16. MacLean, AS & Corner, J 2000, Taking Measures Across the American Landscape, Yale University Press, New Haven, p. 54.

17. Camus, A 1991, The Myth of Sisyphus and Other Essays, J. O'Brien (trans), Vintage Books, New York.

18. Ibid 1.

19. Ibid 2.

20. Ibid 16.

21. Ibid 16, p. 23.

22. van de Graaff & Associates, a. G. A. b. G. S. C. o. J 2009, 'Narrawong Town Report', <http://www.glenelg.vic.gov.au/files/Narrawong_Town_Report.pdf>.

23. Ibid.

24. Simon, J 2013, 'Neomaterialism', <http://www.e-flux.com/journal/20/67643/neo-materialism-part-i-the-commodity-and-the-exhibition/>.

25. Ibid 6.

26. Ibid 6, p. 20.

Opposite:
Site as matter.

Narrative is thus a way of working with 'the material agency or effectivity of non-human or not-quite- human things' opened up by new-materialism.[27] Questioning that perhaps the mode of addressing site as separate from the human – found in contemporary architecture – is no longer valid? That in order to come to an approach to site in the posthuman we need a rethinking of the system of thought through which we approach it and a rearrangement of the hierarchy of materials in which site is regarded. The idea of process, and its subsequent connotation with the word movement, becomes important for this approach where I am drawing parallels between site as process and the way Francesco Careri speaks of walking in his Walkscapes text. Careri described walking as a 'means by which to investigate and unveil...those parts that elude planned control and constitute the unexpressed, untranslatable components in traditional representations'.[28]

Process is thus a way of understanding all materials in site as active in its making. For when all parts are regarded as moving they are all regarded as having a relational effect on each other, and no one part is thought of as being the force from which all else unfolds.

The landscape architect in the posthuman

It is this approach that forms the testing of the method in Narrawong: an engagement with materials across scales as a process of site formation through their displacement within their context. I have chosen to use human labour as a means of displacing these materials, as a critique on the traditional image of the human as separate from site,[29] and as a way of placing the human alongside materials in the formation of site. The material I am looking at to anchor this project is stone, following the work of Eisenman and Derrida in Chora L Works[30] mentioned earlier. Stone has been chosen as it is a material with connotations of the 'ground' (aligning to the contemporary view of site as a surface that I intend to break) and it is a material that readily communicates its context as it is formed by it. By this I mean that stone in particular reflects weathering well, whilst still maintaining its structural integrity (up until a point) and as such is able to be a recorder of site as a process across a time scale that goes beyond that of the individual. Every eighty-three years[31] seven rocks, reflecting the geology types in Narrawong,[32] are displaced from locations across the town and moved to the edge of the Surry River. Through generations more and more rocks are moved, becoming monuments of site through time at the fluctuating river mouth. Over the years, rocks decay and are marked by the river's flux, some becoming submerged while others are revealed by changes in the water level over generations. Through this action the rocks become representative of site in the posthuman, homage to process over outcome in an understanding of site-as- matter. I shall end on the role of landscape architecture in the posthuman which is fundamentally that of the communication of process and change at time scales beyond that of the human. For it is only through embracing change that we are able to move beyond the traditional notions of site as a mark of separation between the human and the material, towards a scaleless non-site that extends the influence of site to all things. It is in this embrace that design projects are able to not only solve problems born from the view of a separate human and non-human world, but also ask questions of the world around us.

Change is fundamental, and because I believe that if one were convinced of the reality of change and if one made an effort to grasp it, everything would become simplified, philosophical difficulties, considered insurmountable, would fall away – I mean the impression things make upon us and the reaction of our intelligence, or sensibility and our will upon things – would perhaps be transformed and, as it were, transfigured. The point is that usually we look at change, but we do not see it. We speak of change, but we do not think about it. We say change exists, that everything changes, that change is the very law of things: yes, we say it and we repeat it, but those are only words, and we reason and philosophise as though change did not exist.[33]

27. Ibid 1.

28. Careri, F 2002, Walkscapes: Walking as an Aesthetic Practice, Gili, Barcelona.

29. Ibid 1.

30. Ibid 2.

31. A time scale derived from the rate of decay of clay soil at an area the size of Mt Clay. Being that every eighty three years 1.2% (the rate at which clay decays) of the volume of the material of Mt Clay undergoes a transformation of matter.

32. Ibid 22.

33. Pearson, KA & Maoilearca, J (eds) 2002, Henri Bergson: Key Writings, Bloomsbury, London.

Opposite top:
Site as Palimpsest.

Opposite bottom:
Geologic Materials.

28 February 1960
28 August 2004
28 November 1985
.28m - 0.5m
28 February 1960
9 October 2002
28 August 2004
.28m ; 0.5m
1 March 2010
3 April 2010
2 January 2014
28 August 2004
14 September 2007
1 January 2012
9 October 2002
October 2002

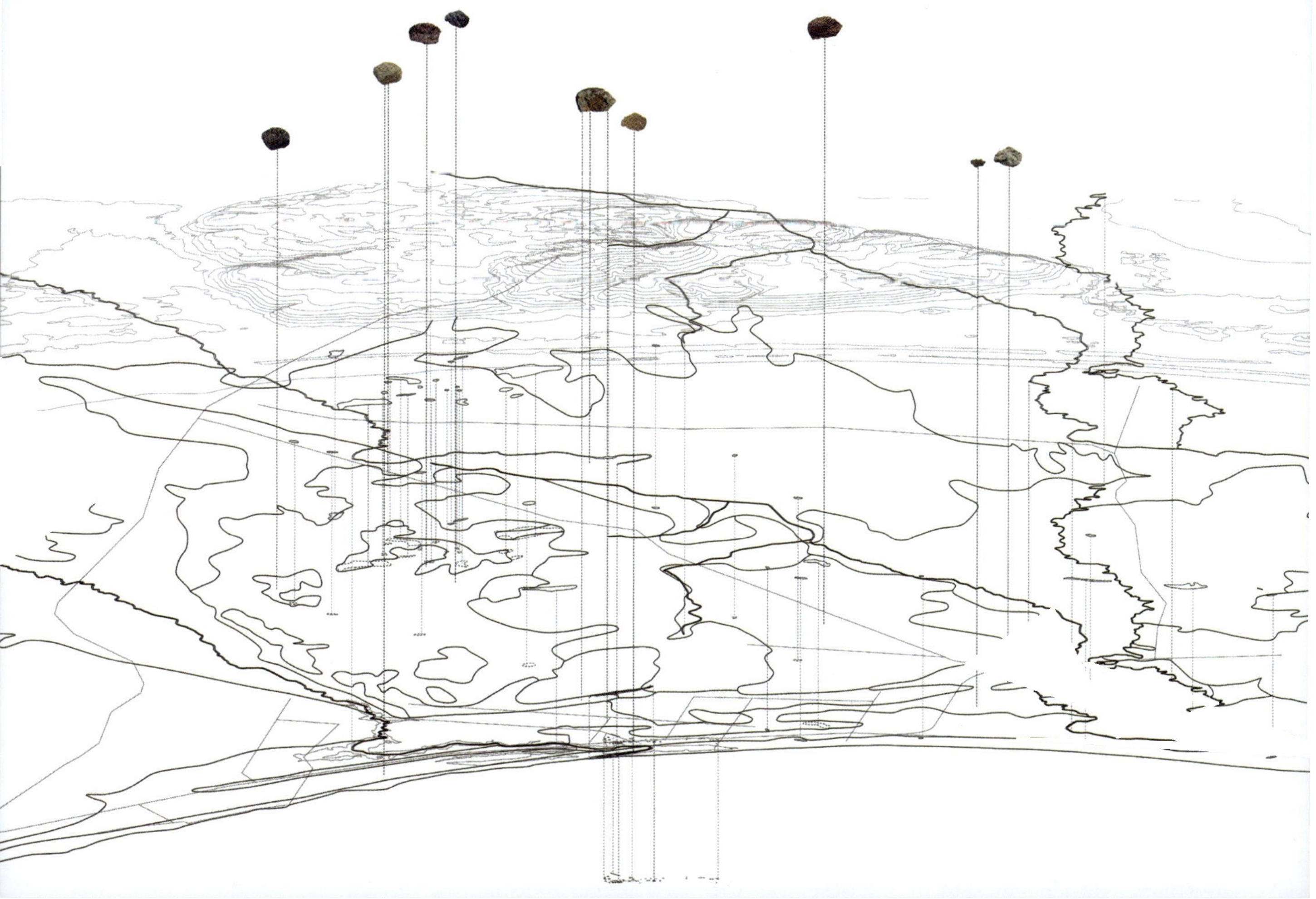

Sara Dean

:

PROTEST AND ASSEMBLY IN THE AUGMENTED CITY

The city and the overlay

The city is a built environment, constructed of metal, glass, and concrete. It is also built of frequencies, signals, and protocols, directly connecting built objects and occupants and allowing them to respond to each other. Through these technologies, the city is becoming a more machine-readable place, and devices are allowing us to access geospatial and proximate data as we move through our environment. As our cities become more augmented, so do our civic actions - assembly, broadcast, and protest.

As the city becomes data-enabled and responsive, new modes of geo engagement are emerging; augmented reality overlays geofences, real-time reporting, public broadcasting, air rights classifications. Infrastructure, traffic, hobbies, schedules, food, finances, and jobs are responding to augmented urban information. And the question of 'to what end' is often being answered by the companies with the most investment in the technology. As the built city is a place of capital fluidity, so too are the augmented technologies of the city; driving apps get us to our destinations in the most efficient routes; Uber calculates surge rates in real-time based on momentary supply and demand; companies target us based on both demography and location.

Like the physical city, though, augmented technologies can be used for other interests than capital generation. The protests, barricades, occupations, sanctuaries, and broadcasts of our cities have their digital counterparts. Data layers are not inert or neutral entities, and in treating them as such, they are more likely to be used as political actors of the systems and power structures that created them. In taking protest to non-physical arenas, we must include data overlays embedded in and on top of the environment with our civic and architectural tools.

Layers and exposure

Augmented reality (AR) is a generalised term describing data overlays on a physical object or place. Watching the traffic change on a road through Google Maps is an augmented reality experience, as is a voucher popping up on your phone when you are close to the relevant business, or collecting Pokémon in an app-based game as you walk through a city. Augmented reality is often viewed as a 'digital window' through a phone, merging the physical environment with digital information. This can include information about natural environments, commercial and retail spaces, and games, fantasies, and other abstract environments.

Augmented realities often expose aspects of our world that we don't expect, and sometimes that the technology doesn't expect. Border Memorial: Frontera de los Muertos, an installation by artist John Craig Freeman in 2012, reveals the locations where people have died crossing the US-Mexico border.[1] This work is a 1:1 memorial in the desert, viewable through Layar or Google Earth: a visceral experience of a data layer and an emergency not otherwise visible on the landscape.

As people roamed cities worldwide, clustering on street corners, parks, and landmarks to play Pokémon GO on their phones, the augmented city was brought into focus (even if the augmentation, in this case, was a city full of cartoon creatures) - and with it an implicit social agreement was exposed. As Pokémon GO players wandered around in search

1. Freeman, JC 2016, 'Border Memorial: Frontera de los Muertos', <https://johncraigfreeman.wordpress.com/border-memorial-frontera-de-los-muertos/>.

2. Women's March 2017, 'Sister Marches', <https://www.womensmarch.com/sisters>.

3. Lacambra, S 2016, 'Investigating Law Enforcement's Possible Use of Surveillance Technology at Standing Rock', Electronic Frontier Foundation, <https://www.eff.org/deeplinks/2016/12/investigating-law-enforcements-use-technology-surveil-and-disrupt-nodapl-water>.

4. Davidson, C & de Leon, M P 2016, 'The Architectural Imagination', <http://www.thearchitecturalimagination.org/>.

5. Detroit Resists 2016, 'Statement on the US Pavilion at the 2016 Venice Architecture Biennale', <https://detroitresists.org/2016/02/20/statement-on-the-u-s-pavilion-at-the-2016-venice-architecture-biennale/>.

Top:
Detroit Resists
View of Digital Occupation of the US Pavilion, Detroit Resists, 2016.

of collectible critters, they would gather in memorials and cemeteries, religious sites, and other sacred spaces. The game was programmed to use public spaces and landmarks for locations, without differentiating based on the type of public landmark. Public outcry over gaming in these places resulted in the gamemakers eventually creating a global dataset of sacred spaces to be eliminated from the game's collection zones: a set of areas AR had exposed to view.

Area denial/data denial

The use of social media and digital community platforms as means for community organisation - from organising coordinated public events, to consolidating political movements, to documenting evidence of brutality - has been well documented. The effectiveness of the Women's Marches on January 21st, 2017, in the end comprising 637 simultaneous events, stands as evidence of the efficacy of these tools to create coordinated, independent global events with the same associated branding, message, and memes.[2]

But another way to calculate the value of a technology is to look at the attempts to control and limit access to it. The protest at Standing Rock in North Dakota has become a legislative touch point of the ways to limit digital access, confuse augmented space, and control digital experiences of protest by attacking devices and access points. Protesters experienced chronic lost data, deleted posts, lack of signal, drained batteries, and overheating phones. The Electronic Frontier Foundation's investigation of these accounts points to the potential use of CSSs (cell-site simulators), which act as a cell tower and collect or interfere with cell data of any phone in the area.[3] Regardless of which technologies were used to intercept the protesters data, the symptoms are evidence of the importance of digital broadcasting and documentation as civic tools.

Digital occupation

The call for the 2016 US Pavilion in the Venice Biennale, The Architectural Imagination, asked for 'new speculative architectural projects' for Detroit, emphasising the 'value of the architectural imagination in shaping forms and spaces into exciting future possibilities'.[4] Large-scale interventions were emphasised by the iconic sites chosen by the curators throughout the city. The Detroit community, though, especially the activist community, felt under attack by the call and the curation of the projects for the US Pavilion. This threat was in particular a response to the similarity between the call and local events - the city was in the process of large scale land consolidation by developers, helped by new city policies redefining blight and eviction. By taking on the characteristics of the developer community, The Architectural Imagination, intentionally or not, was embodying this city threat.

Detroit Resists, a collection of Detroit-area activists and architects, formed to give local voice to the opposition of this project.[5] I worked with Detroit Resists to find a technological means to be 'present' at the Biennale and add their voice to the conversation about Detroit's future. Augmented reality allowed Detroit Resists to create a digital installation on the US Pavilion's geo-coordinates. This 'digital occupation' used new technologies to build on the physical traditions of sit-ins and physical protests, adding activist installations from Detroit directly into the Pavilion without impeding the physical exhibit. The Biennale was flyered, physically and via social media, with information about how to see the Digital Occupation of the US Pavilion. Media picked up the story, with photos of the exhibition layered with digital objects from the Occupation; a graffitied water tower, or an anti-eviction mural on a home fence. Through a layered spatial experience, the community was able to be on-the-ground at the Biennale.

The digital civic body

The history of speculative and 'paper' architecture is a history of the ways that we can envision new relationships between people and their environment, or new power systems or value sets of future civilisations. Technologies are similarly offering new visions of future worlds, with responsive data and closer relationships between people and the built environment. But the real test of our agency to impact the future is in our ability to use technology itself as a platform for experimentation, protest, and contestation. What are the speculative futures we can envision through the tools at hand and the increasing augmentation of our built world?

New technologies are often lent to solidify existing power structures – to virtually tour luxury condos for purchase, or convince investors of the potential of a future development. But like all tools, and architecture for that matter, they do not embody a politic through their existence, but through their use. It is our responsibility as architects and designers of cities to see augmentation as a civic device as well as a commercial one. And ask ourselves the futures we are implying through the ways we deploy them in our work.

Detroit Map
Map of augmented installation.
Digital Occupation of the US Pavilion catalogue, Detroit Resists. Venice, Italy. 2016.

Opposite top:
View of Border Memorial: Frontera de los Muertos, John Craig Freeman, augmented reality public art. Southern Arizona, USA. 2012 – Present.

Opposite bottom:
Detroit Resists
View of Digital Occupation of the US Pavilion, Detroit Resists. Venice, Italy. 2016.

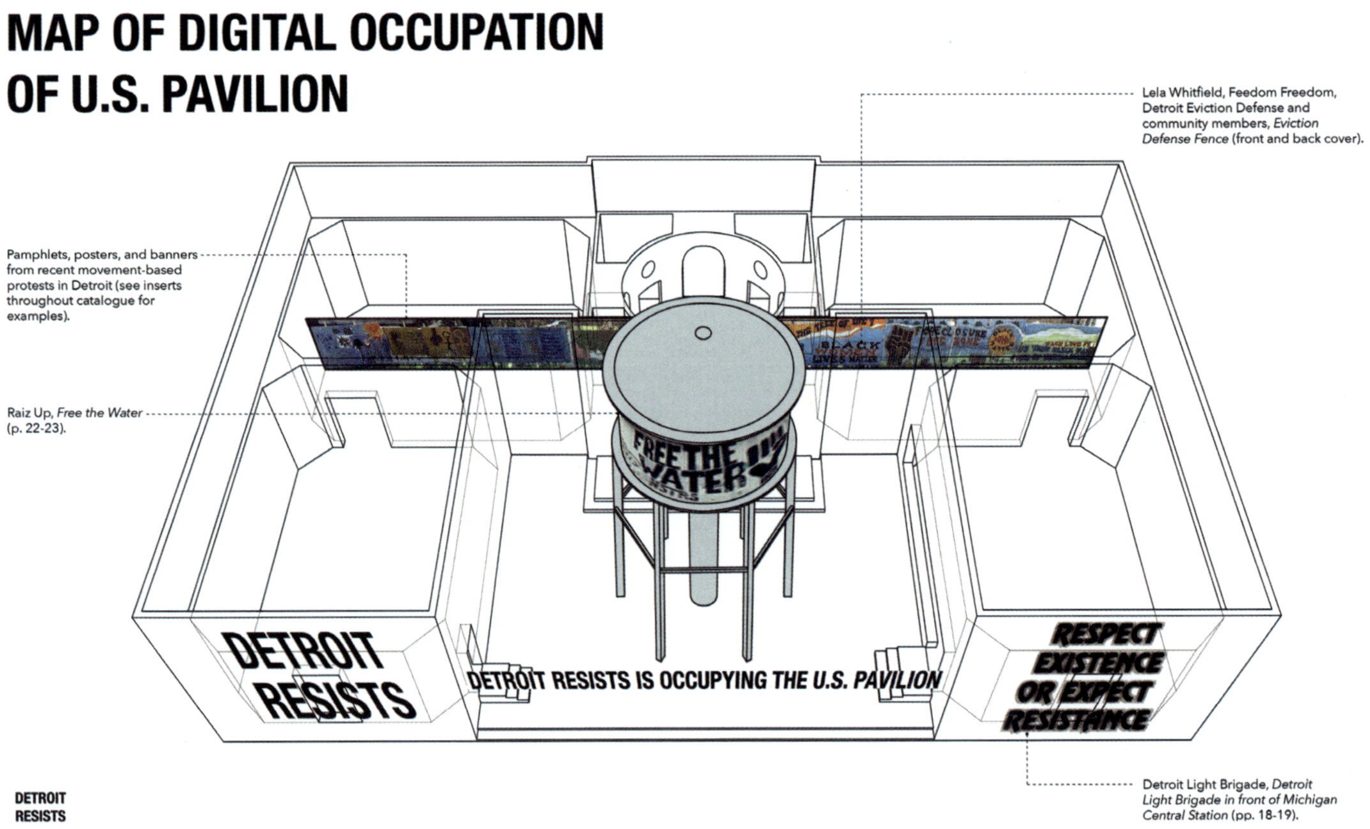

htc 
T-Mobile
DET
DETROIT
RESISTS

Anatol Pitt

ENFOLDED

I've been taking close-up photographs of charcoal drawings on Japanese paper. The lens is used to collapse scale and construct landscapes in a way that can be both immense and intimate. This interest in surface emerges from the way, as one gets closer, the boundaries begin to blur and the spaces open up. In this way, audiences are invited to see the 'constructedness' of things as well as finding new ways of seeing and thinking about them.

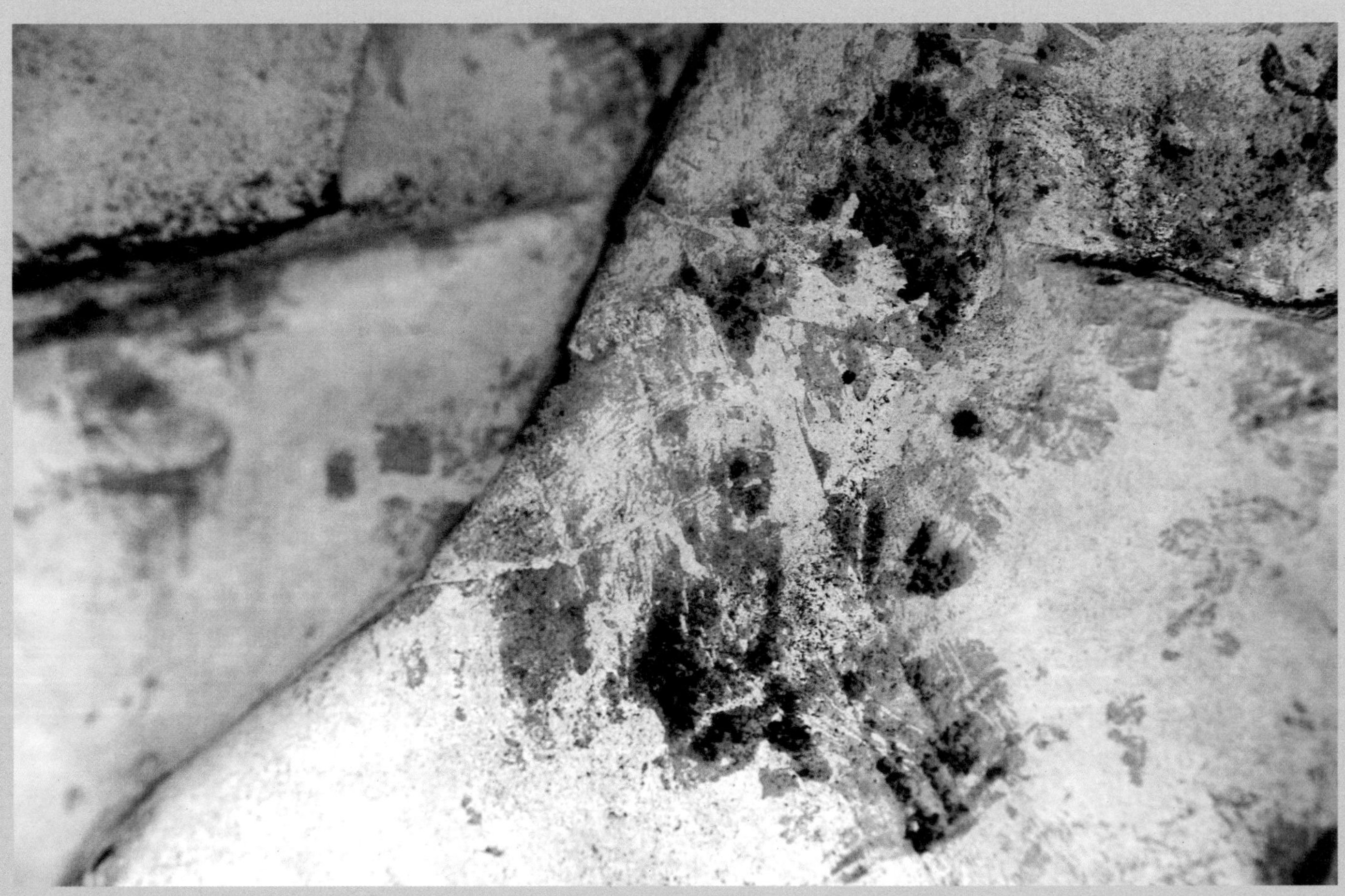

TanDEM-X 2016, from Enfolded
Pigment inkjet print on archival paper
1100 x 770mm

Opposite:
Flux 2016, from Enfolded
Pigment inkjet print on archival paper
1100 x 770mm

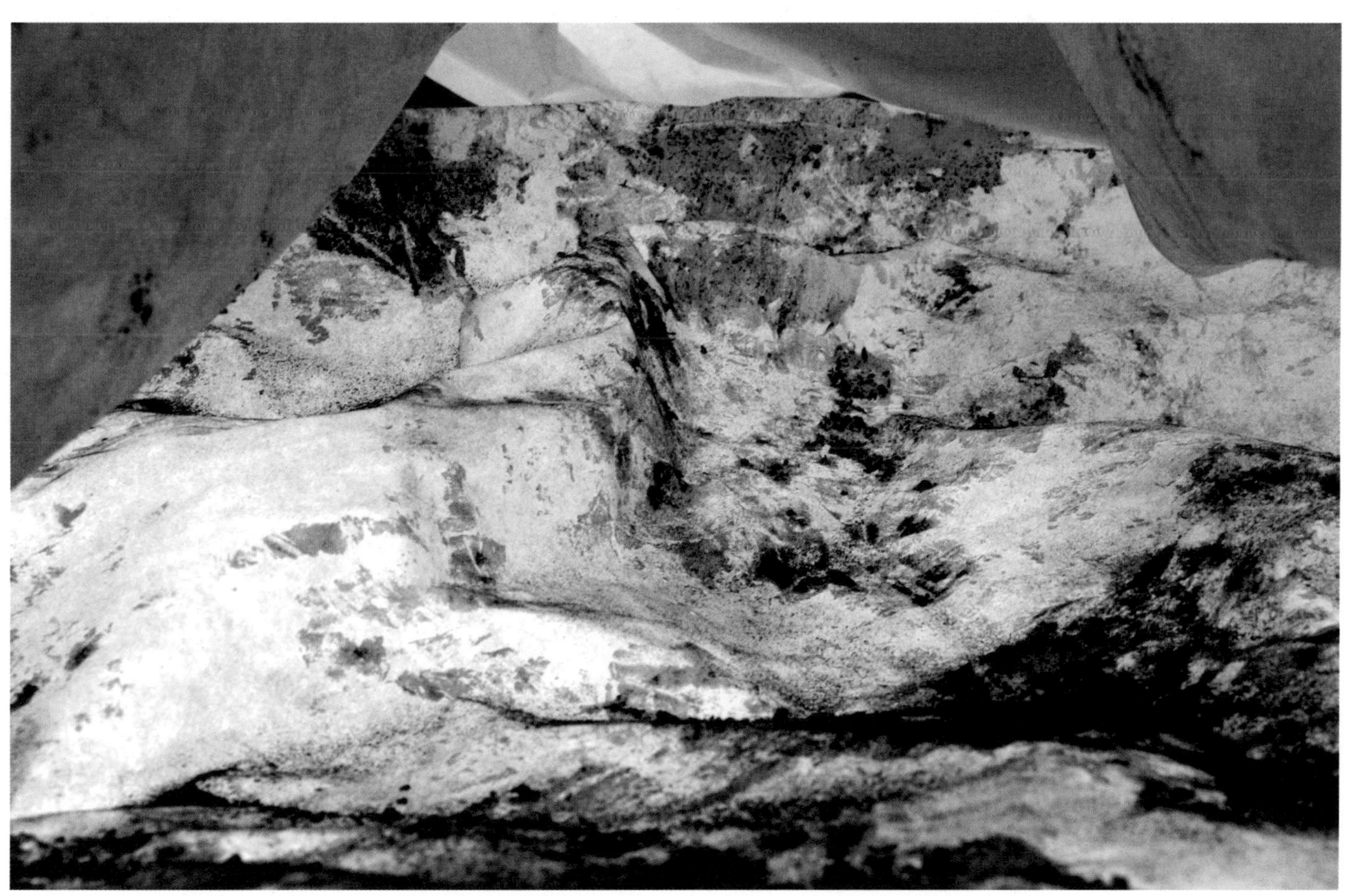

NICHOLAS REBSTADT

:

POST-TRUTH OR PRE-COLLECTIVE IMAGINATION: NOTES ON SHIFTY TRUTH, DESIGN AND REAL KARDASHIANS

Design and Kim Kardashian have something in common. They both blur fiction with reality. The definition of 'post-truth' is still in formation. It is still a buzzword and arguably a long way from solidifying, if ever, but its relationship to design is an interesting one, primarily because fiction and truth have never been closer to one another, and designers work with both.

Post-truth implies there was or is a 'truth' to begin with, but what is contemporary authenticity and truth? 'Post' suggests there was a period, the good old days, where design was real. This 'truth' in design tacitly implies its authenticity. Here, the authentic or truthful nature of design practices to develop and pilot change consequentially comes under threat, as without a 'truth' authentic design can no longer be measured in the way that we understand it to be measured – as having the ability to affect change positively.

The implication is that we need to understand truth in a more fluid way. This 'precession of simulacra' has replaced the information that we know as 'truth', as concrete, referent, or fact.[1] 'Abstraction today is no longer that of the map, the double, the mirror or the concept. Simulation is no longer that of a territory, a referential being or a substance.'[2] Authentic authenticity – if there ever was such a thing – departed this world decades ago. Jean Baudrillard outlines the disconnection of the signifier to the signified or concrete referent. This abstracted simulation is no longer tied to 'a territory, a referential being or a substance' and this is important because this fundamental relationship – if we assume that the alignment of the signified or simulacra with the referent equates to 'truth' or 'authenticity' as it is conventionally understood – is no longer there, only simulated.[3]

In the sphere of post-truth the hyperreal is something that considers its end over the means, its goal over its substance. We know truth or reality is disingenuous from the very beginning. It has a commercial aim, an ulterior motive. It is indeed, fictional. Truth is no longer in the authenticity of the referent but in the value and impact of the communication or signified, which is now everything.

Nobody watches Keeping up with the Kardashians expecting to see 'real' lives, only a simulation of how we imagine them, and this is enough. Truth is not important here, just the signification of it. The genre of reality television is less about realness than it is about the communication of reality. In the process of communication, the reality has become confected and fictionalised. This fluid atmospheric shift has contributed to a cynicism that has cultivated an ecology that conceptually supports post-truth.

French collective, Tiqqun, propose a framework for the commodification of the individual into 'living capital' through the model Young-Girl.[5] For them, the young girl is the ideal metaphor for consumption and complicity under capitalism: young, slightly naïve and eternally youthful. The young girl is the model citizen, the ideal consumer complicit in the commodification and production-consumption of information. This very information, this exchange of information between people, is important. With the continual comparison of oneself to another, the domination of the status quo continues as there is no room for true contention. There is no other choice apart from what is already on offer, and what is on offer is not inspirational for change.

The Young-Girl conceives liberty as the possibility of choosing from among a thousand insignificances.[4] Crucially, this flow of information - of simulation - can be coded and commodified; bought, sold and traded in a marketplace that is streamlined in its meanings out of necessity. The less abstract the meaning of the code or message the faster it can be interpreted, commodified and consumed in an information economy.

Market-centred thinking around how cities are planned, developed and lived in are projected through the way that cities are read, branded and conceptualised in relation to one another. These narratives are produced intricately by designers for people and the market backing them, acutely realised on an interior scale through property development. No new development not exists without a plan and a series of renders. These renders reinforce the normalisation of neoliberal market values through the communication of signifieds that cultivate a particular lifestyle narrative within the city. It is not coincidental that all bathroom renders look like they are plentifully stocked with Aesop. Crafting these narratives is something that folds into a larger mythology of urban space and the city.

With the context of many luxury apartments, there is a delightful complexity in how these renders curate the grunge appeal of the existing neighbourhood with the luxury of minimalism that these developments often signify. Gentrification can never be removed from a city, but it should not have absolute dominance. Narratives of 'politically inert' residential design, in this sense, are highly political and work to produce an urban space to the ends of a marketed, purchasable 'creative' lifestyle. Renders like this reinforce the current cultural mythologies apparent in the design world and they also have the potential to become subverted through fictional narratives.

The single largest strength of the current neoliberal narratives is their monopoly over the collective intellect. These narratives are strong because there is no challenging, disruptive or destabilising narrative for the way spaces are designed, produced and lived in. Fiction can operate in this area by cultivating and re-imagining these narratives where designers play a decisive role.

This ubiquitous narrative provides the economic stability that capital is reliant on to provide 'jobs and growth'. However, this contrived consensus works to undermine the political within space by eliminating contention and competition - ironic really, given its emphasis on markets. It is this apparatus that is instrumental in the development and growth of cities and the reinforcing of the overarching paradigms that form mythologies and fictions of the urban experience.

There is a level of tension where designers operate between the fictional and propositional, brushing against the pragmatic needs of a concrete reality - within the milieu of the informational. Designers are the planners and tools from which these fictions are written, and consequently can also be contested. Designers are uniquely aware of how the urban functions, how it feels and how its future might unfold. We are visionaries whose heroic desire for transformation, once emphatically state-sanctioned, is now hostage to codefied market forces.[6] When designers propose a design they

1. Baudrillard, J 1994, Simulacra and Simulation, University of Michigan Press, Ann Arbor, Michigan, United States, p. 169.

2. Ibid 1.

3. Ibid 1.

4. Tiqqun 2012, Preliminary Materials for a Theory of the Young-Girl, Reines, A (trans), Semiotext(e), Los Angeles, California, United States, p. 100.

5. Ibid 4.

6. Also combined with the often precarious position of designing in the first place.

7. I use the term 'spatial design' intentionally to not only include landscape architects, urban designers and architects, but also interior designers, app developers, Instagram users and anyone else who directly engages with the contemporary conditions of the urban on a daily basis.

8. Blast Theory 2016, 'Operation Black Antler', <http://www.blasttheory.co.uk/projects/operation-black-antler/>.

9. Goldin, S & Senneby, J 2008, 'Looking for Headless, Goldin & Senneby', <http://www.alphagalileo.org/AssetViewer.aspx?AssetId=32996&CultureCode=en>.

have a vision for what the future is because they are literally commissioned to design it, they have an awareness of the codes and conventions that facilitate these fictions.

It's a cliché to refer to the world as 'connected', but it is. Cities are elaborate compositions of legitimate and informal phenomena that are both concrete, social, economic and informational. Information flows through the city as freely as the people passing through its streets. Contemporary spatial design not only engages with the flow of information and data on an empirical level to design, but additionally what is designed adds to the ecology that it draws from.[7] This aesthetically attractive idea gives purpose to many designers. This choreographic flow of information in relation to the materialisation of space is codified and communicated efficiently. Any ambiguity, contradiction or outlier is normalised as soon as possible.

A falsification

It is through this ambiguity and vagueness that the potential in fictional disruption lies. Operation Black Antler, an immersive theatre work from Brighton-based group Blast Theory directly utilises the spatial conditions of Brighton for narrative effect, weaving a narrative themed around surveillance issues and alt-right actions.[8] The work itself is one of many on a similar overture from the UK-based collective which examine these issues through blurring the lines of fiction and reality.

In the performance, you are invited to an address via text message. You appear at the flat, fumbling for the correct buzzer as the sun sets, it's getting cold and the harsh fluorescent lighting at the tower-block foyer is still yet to switch on. Once inside you are, in a characteristically English way, offered a cup of tea and invited to take a seat in a modest yet tidy living room. From there, an emphatic (yet ultimately convincing) project leader reveals the beginning of the performance narrative which places you as part of a covert operation against the alt-right English Defence League (EDL). Everyone is asked to develop a cover story about who they are and where they have come from, before proceeding into the rest of the play where the boundaries of who is and is not part of the play blur completely.

Operation Black Antler uses politically contested urban space, nuanced knowledge of local anthropologies, and culture to develop a narrative that is - crucially - based in information flows and fragments that are drawn from media, and offers a choice in how we respond and perhaps even reclaim public spaces. It does so by crafting a careful fiction that is, in itself, immersive and playful. Here the line between reality and play is blurred. Like most immersive theatre or urban gaming, it latches parasitically to the systems that support it, subverting meaning through the craft of fiction. These systems being the immediate geographical context and the geopolitical. Operation Black Antler is distinctly English in tone and context however it also opens issues that transcend the borders of their union and nation generally. These are globalised issues, and are applicable across many contexts.

> *He looks at the book, puzzled. His own novel, published a few years ago and already a distant memory to him. Even his name on the cover looks wrong, an imposition, a mistake, a falsification.*[9]

Post-truth marginalises the necessity of truth. It does not eliminate the desire for it. In doing so, it opens up possibilities of disrupting and altering the very certainties that are now commodified and traded on a social marketplace. The thoughts of John Barlow, a character in the novel Looking for Headless authored by fictional writer 'KD' are quoted above. Looking for Headless (the novel) forms part of a greater web of information that weaves into the larger work of Swedish conceptual artists Simon Goldin and Jakob Senneby (Goldin+Senneby). The larger work, Headless, is both a novel and an artwork that simultaneously functions as a fictionalised spatial proposition ranging from Europe to the offshore financial centres of the Caribbean.

Goldin+Senneby do not make public appearances. They almost always 'appear' through emissaries in rented, global corporate spaces like Regus offices, galleries and lecture spaces. The artist's voice is asserted by a team of 'experts' in the fields of globalisation (Angus Cameron, publishing; KD published by Triple Canopy) and the world of art encountered through exhibitions - Power to the People at ACCA, for instance. The work produced for exhibition is fractal at best, and above all non-prescriptive. It often includes excerpts of audio and literature that the individual struggles to define or place as 'authentic'.

Headless is not centred on the distribution of virtual information, it simply uses this flow and collection of information as a vehicle to deliver a narrative. This narrative is a chain of information pieced together by the subjectivity and judgement of the viewer, creating a space of contention in and of itself. In Headless, Goldin+Senneby craft a chain of meaning, connecting them to each other and the occasional referent (authority) of 'truth', such as a publishing house, academic or conference venue and gallery. The development of fiction can be disrupted to produce alternative truths, knowledge and conflict, which is essential in the production of a truly politicised space. None of these alternative truths is the truth. The plot is nebulous and is in many ways futile to relay here; it is beside the point. The destabilisation of this narrative authority is something that is critical in this work, and in a fictional disruptive strategy. The work expressly questions our encounter with truth, with the production of contemporary subjectivity and conflict, which is precisely why it is relevant to spatial design practices.

In subverting and undermining the mythologies that form a solidified narrative and appear as truth in public space, design can develop fictions that offer a space of contention in the often uncontested neoliberal myths of urban space. In doing so, design can revive collective imagination that can not only disrupt the status quo, but also use post-truth itself as a tool to produce a contested imagining of space. To do this however, designers must start with their practices and the narratives that shape their very own identity and commercial praxis.

AUSTRALIAN INSTITUTE OF LANDSCAPE ARCHITECTS (AILA)

AILA's Connection to Country Committee, Victoria, provides advice to the Victorian Chapter Executive of AILA on the design and delivery of the Connection to Country Strategy in the State of Victoria. The committee contributes to setting the agenda for the AILA Victoria Connection to Country Strategy; assists in establishing relationships of AILA with Victorian Aboriginal leaders and groups; assists AILA Victoria in advocating for better engagement with, and representation of, Indigenous Connection to Country understanding and traditions; advises on Indigenous student engagement, attraction and retention; and makes recommendations on the Connection to Country Strategy to the Victorian Chapter Executive. The committee is led by Anne-Marie Pisani, an RLA with a lifelong passion for Indigenous cultures.

AJNA BABAHMETOVIC

Ajna Babahmetovic was born in 1992 in Zenica in Bosnia and, after finishing high school, decided to study architecture in Graz in 2011. After one year of learning German, Ajna started studying at TU Graz (Graz University of Technology). Ajna is now doing Masters-level Architecture studies and working in an architecture office.

JULIAN DAY

Julian Day is an artist, composer, writer and broadcaster. He co-directs Super Critical Mass in which temporary communities articulate public spaces with dispersed homogeneous sound. Julian has presented work at the 2017 California-Pacific Triennial (Orange County Museum of Art), Bang On A Can Marathon, MATA Festival, Huddersfield Contemporary Music Festival, Royal Academy of Music, Prague Quadrennial of Performance Design and Space, Eighth Asia Pacific Triennial of Contemporary Art (Queensland Gallery of Modern Art), Australian Centre for Contemporary Art, Institute of Modern Art, MONA FOMA and Liquid Architecture. He has had work acquired by the Museum of Contemporary Art Australia. Julian has appeared extensively on ABC and BBC radio.

SARA DEAN

Sara Dean is Assistant Professor at California College of the Arts in San Francisco. Her work considers the implications of emerging technologies on public engagement, urban interface and 'smart' cities. Her research studio, VUCA, designs urban strategies to engage complex systems and uncertain futures. This work spans spatial and digital media, with a commitment to open-access data and crowd-production.

JASON HO

Jason Ho is a curator, urbanist and educator. He is an initiator of Mapping for Humanity in China and a founding member of South China Association of Landscape Architecture (SCALA). Jason has taught, researched and practiced at a large number of universities and design firms across the globe. Jason received a PhD of Landscape Architecture from RMIT University in 2014, in which his creative design research was focused on the mapping of lived experiences around boundary walls in China. After his PhD completion, Jason embarked on a thesis dissemination tour. He has now led thirty-five mapping workshops and delivered over 100 talks at different universities and design institutions worldwide. Jason was the sub-curator of the 2017 Shenzhen & Hong Kong Bi-City Biennale of Urbanism\Architecture. He is currently teaching at the School of Architecture at South China University of Technology, Guangzhou.

HOTHAM STREET LADIES

The Hotham Street Ladies are a group of five women who, at one time, lived in a shared household in Collingwood. They still draw much inspiration from this household, including their love of food, dinner parties, domestic landscapes, CWA cookbooks and sense of community. The Hotham Street Ladies' work embraces the themes of food, fashion, feminism and craft. Their work examines how their collaborative participation in, and contemporising of, these activities creates their own distinct cultural community and connects to others. The Hotham Street Ladies combine innovation and contemporary critique with nostalgic or familiar elements that are accessible to a wide audience.
The Hotham Street Ladies are Cassandra Chilton, Molly O'Shaughnessy, Sarah Parkes, Caroline Price and Lyndal Walker.

JESS JOHNSON

Jess Johnson was born in Tauranga, New Zealand, in 1979. In 2016, after twelve years of living and working in Melbourne, Australia, she relocated permanently to New York. Jess's drawing and installation practice is influenced by the speculative intersections across language, science fiction, culture and technology. Jess's work has been exhibited in Australia and New Zealand as well as internationally. She has participated in solo and group exhibitions at Jack Hanley Gallery, New York; Art Basel, Hong Kong; Talbot Rice Gallery, Edinburgh; National Gallery of Victoria, Australia; Museum of Contemporary Art, Australia; and Christchurch Art Gallery, New Zealand.

KASIA KEELEY

Kasia Keeley is a 2017 graduate of the University of Washington Master of Landscape Architecture program. She has a Bachelor of Fine Arts in Printmaking and has focused her graduate education on the remediation and re-engagement of post-industrial landscapes through ecological and artistic programming. In late 2016 she received the Valle Fellowship to conduct research in Scandinavia regarding the ecological and social impacts of post-industrial and nuclear sites and their role within heritage discourse. Kasia has given presentations on her research at Södertörn University in Sweden and at the 2017 conference of the American Society of Landscape Architects, Washington Chapter. She has been invited to speak at Nuclear Legacies: Community, Memory, Waste and Nature in Stockholm in late 2017. She will be entering into landscape architecture practice after graduating and is looking forward to combining her research in brownfields, agriculture and art with local projects.

ASA KREMMER

Asa is currently studying a Master of Landscape Architecture at RMIT University. He recently completed an internship with Stoss Landscape Urbanism in Boston, USA. Asa studied abroad at Delft University of Technology in the Netherlands, where he applied architectural engineering solutions to a major port off the coast of Rotterdam. Building on his previous studies, Asa has conducted research in Guangzhou and Copenhagen and in several domestic sites, and his work has been featured in publications in Melbourne and Hong Kong. He is a designer who is fascinated by mapping political systems and their impact on the built environment.

KARL KULLMAN

Karl Kullmann is a landscape architect, urban designer and tenured Associate Professor at the University of California, Berkeley, where he teaches design studios in landscape architecture and urban design and courses in landscape theory and digital modelling. Karl's research and creative work covers a wide range of subjects including rural and urban decline, urban topography, green infrastructure, urban wastelands, public gardens, spatial orientation and mapping, and design modelling visualisation. These topics are actively tested through Karl's design practice, which includes constructed urban landscape projects in China, Australia and Germany, and numerous design competition prizes and exhibitions.

KEES LOKMAN

Kees Lokman is an Assistant Professor of Landscape Architecture at the University of British Columbia. He holds degrees in planning, urban design and landscape architecture. His writing and academic research, which focuses on the intersection of landscape, infrastructure and ecology, has been published in various journals, including Journal of Landscape Architecture, The Journal of Architectural Education, Topos, Landscapes/Paysages and New Geographies. Kees is also the founder of Parallax Landscape, a collaborative and design-based research platform that explores challenges related to water and food shortages, the global energy transition, and climate change adaptation. The work and research produced by Parallax Landscape has received numerous design awards and recognition.

HAYDEN MATTHYS

Hayden Matthys holds a Bachelor of Design (Landscape Architecture) from RMIT University and is currently completing his Master of Landscape Architecture, also at RMIT. Hayden has a passion for prompting viewer curiosity through design, which has led to design research projects both in Victoria and abroad. He was a co-editor of issue 24 of Kerb Journal of Landscape Architecture and has been published online by Landscape Australia Magazine.

ALEXANDRA MEI

Alexandra Mei produces work that addresses the social, material and political influences of landscape architecture on daily life. Alexandra graduated with distinction from the Harvard University Graduate School of Design (GSD) with a Master in Landscape Architecture, after receiving a Bachelor of Design in Architecture from Washington University in St. Louis. While at the GSD, Alexandra served as the co-chair for the school's Women in Design organisation, guiding projects advocating and celebrating gender equity and diversity in the design profession. She has received several honours including the GSD Thesis Award in Landscape Architecture and 2017 Charles Eliot Traveling Fellowship from the GSD.

EMMA MENDEL

Emma Mendel is a Canadian landscape architect practising, researching and writing about materiality, representation and cultural-infrastructural landscapes. She obtained her Master of Landscape Architecture from the University of Toronto after completing her Bachelor of Fine Arts at the Rhode Island School of Design. In her project, Emma's research lies at the chasm between planned water systems and the cultural usage of water. This liminal space is situated in existing conditions with proposed infrastructural solutions, a strategy to protect the sacred. As a medium of communications, representation is concurrently explored as a means to share the mutability of the medium of water.

GEAN MORENO

Gean Moreno is Curator of Programs at the Institute of Contemporary Art (ICA) Miami, where he founded and organises the Art + Research Center. He is on the Advisory Board of the 2017 Whitney Biennial and serves as co-director of [NAME] Publications. Between 2014 and 2016, Gean was Artistic Director at Cannonball, where he developed pedagogical platforms and public commissions. He has contributed texts to various catalogues and publications, including e-flux journal, Kaleidoscope, and Art in America, and has lectured at numerous universities.

ERNESTO OROZA

Ernesto Oroza is an artist, designer and author based in South Florida. A graduate of Havana's Superior Institute of Design and later a professor in both Havana and Paris, his practice is geared to highlighting and critically understanding man-object interactions and the role that collective engagements with material culture have in the making of community. He is the author of several books on popular creativity as expressed in tool objects and the urban environment – what he theorises as 'technological disobedience' and 'architecture of necessity', respectively. Ernesto's creative practice is grounded in community research, and he develops research methods as well as channels of dissemination that follow the vernacular practices and economic logics of his subject-objects. His ultimate goal is to provoke a feedback loop between his findings and the community involved to generate both critical inquiry and positive change.

SUVENDRINI PERERA

Suvendrini Perera is John Curtin Distinguished Professor and Research Professor of Cultural

Studies in the School of Media, Culture and Creative Arts at Curtin University. She has published widely on issues of social justice, including decolonisation, race, ethnicity and multiculturalism, refugee topics, critical whiteness studies and Asian–Australian studies. She has combined her academic career with participation in policymaking, public life and activism. She is the author/editor of seven books, including Reaches of Empire, Australia and the Insular Imagination: Beaches, Borders, Boats and Bodies, and Survival Media: The Politics and Poetics of Mobility and the War in Sri Lanka. Currently she is the lead investigator on two ARC-funded projects: Old Atrocities, New Media; and Deathscapes. With Joseph Pugliese, she is a founding member of Researchers Against Pacific Black Sites.

ANATOL PITT

Anatol Pitt is an artist and writer based in Melbourne. He holds a degree in art history and anthropology from the University of Melbourne (2014), and is completing a degree in fine art at the Victorian College of the Arts. Working across a variety of media, often with found and provisional materials, he assembles and reassembles patterns of information to construct new spaces and temporalities. His current body of work explores redocumentation and staged landscapes. The series Enfolded comprises photographic close-ups of drawings on folded paper. This work uses the camera lens to collapse scales and construct a space that is both immense and intimate. Its aesthetic stems from the histories of abstraction, scientific imagery, mapping and exploration. These are fields that try to visualise and model spaces that are unknown or unseeable, yet often sideline their own construction.

ANDREW PRINDLE

Andrew Prindle is a 2017 graduate from the University of Washington's Master of Landscape Architecture program. While at the University of Washington, Andrew served as a teaching and technical assistant for history and studio courses. Andrew's research focuses on the history of places to uncover the conditions and processes of a place's evolving political ecology, particularly where natural systems have been heavily reconfigured by industrial or infrastructural systems. He has worked with Jeff Hou and Sabine Knierbein on two book projects focused on design and democracy. Andrew is one of the original team members of Urban@UW where he was a research assistant and communications coordinator. He also developed the framework and edited reports for the inaugural year of the Livable City Year program at UW.

JOSEPH PUGLIESE

Professor Joseph Pugliese is Research Director of the Department of Media, Music, Communication and Cultural Studies at Macquarie University. His key research areas are: social justice praxis, law, culture and the humanities, colonialism and decoloniality, race, ethnicity and whiteness, refugees and asylum seekers, bodies and technologies, and state violence. His most recent publications include two monographs: Biometrics: Bodies, Technologies, Biopolitics, shortlisted for the Surveillance Studies Book Prize, and State Violence and the Execution of Law: Biopolitical Caesurae of Torture, Black Sites, Drones, nominated for the US Law and Society Book Award and the UK's Hart Socio-Legal Book Prize. His latest book, Forensic Ecologies, will be published by Edinburgh University Press in late 2017. With Suvendrini Perera, he is a founding member of Researchers Against Pacific Black Sites.

NICK REBSTADT

Nick Rebstadt is a freelance designer and sessional lecturer in the Interior Design program at RMIT University. His practice focuses on how contemporary ideas and structures affect design (both positively and negatively), and designers' agency to affect meaningful change. His design interests range from relational gestures to the urban scale, with a particular focus on recent developments in workplace and service design and their impact on contemporary space and interior practice.

GRANT REVELL

Grant Revell is a (non-Indigenous) practising landscape architect, teacher, researcher and Associate Dean of Education at The University of Western Australia's School of Indigenous Studies. His work focuses on landscape architecture's multi-disciplinary role in the health and wellbeing of Indigenous communities. Grant was made a National Fellow of the Australian Institute of Landscape Architects in 2014 for his contributions to Indigenous design education and practice. He currently lives in the old shorelines of the Indian Ocean in North Fremantle.

KHVAY SAMNANG

Khvay Samnang was born in 1982 in Svay Rieng, Cambodia. He graduated from the Painting Department at the Royal University of Fine Arts in the capital Phnom Penh, where he lives and works today. His multidisciplinary practice spans performance, photography, video, installation and sculpture. Prompted by instinct, newsfeeds and rumours, his experiential investigations offer new interpretations of history and contentious current affairs that resist the polarising language known to media and legal reports. Khvay's recent solo exhibitions include Where is My Land? (Sa Sa Art Projects, Phnom Penh), Footprints of Yantra Man (Museum of Contemporary Art, Santa Barbara) and Rubber Man (Jeu de Paume, Paris). Group exhibitions include documenta 14 (EMST, Athens and Ottoneum, Kassel), People, Money, Ghosts (Jim Thompson Art Center, Bangkok), and the Ninth Asia Pacific Triennial of Contemporary Art (Queensland Gallery of Modern Art, Brisbane). Khvay is a member of Stiev Selepak art collective and a co-founder of SA SA BASSAC and Sa Sa Art Projects, where he teaches contemporary art to emerging Cambodian artists.

SHUANG SHUANG WU

Shuang Shuang Wu maintains practice and a research interest in landscape as a setting for social and environmental narratives. She holds a Master of Landscape Architecture with distinction from the University of Illinois at Urbana-Champaign (UIUC). She earned a Field Travel Fellowship from the Department of Landscape Architecture at UIUC, which supported her travel along the Mexico–United States border. Shuangshuang is currently a registered landscape architect based in New York and a senior designer at Hargreaves Associates. She has experience in many public projects ranging from conceptual master plans to precise detailing site design and construction.

ELIZABETH (LIZZIE) YARINA

Elizabeth (Lizzie) Yarina recently completed a joint Master of Architecture and Master of City Planning at MIT, with her thesis entitled POST-ISLAND FUTURES: Design as Agency for Tuvalu's Sinking Atolls. Her research explores the role of design thinking in political and territorial issues, with a particular focus on climate change and natural resources. Prior to attending MIT, Lizzie worked in the field of architectural design at William Rawn Associates in Boston and PLY Architecture in Ann Arbor. She received her Bachelor of Science in Architecture from the University of Michigan in 2010. Lizzie grew up on a sheep farm in Tapiola, Michigan, a sixty-mile drive from Eagle Mine along Keweenaw Bay and through Michigamme forest.

Advertising and Sponsorship

The Kerb production team and the RMIT Landscape Architecture program would like to thank our sponsors for their generous financial support toward this publication.

Patron

Taylor Cullity Lethlean (TCL)

Friends

Sue Barnsley Design
Candalepas Associates

Silent Auction Supporters

Hotham Street Ladies
Lamington Drive
Charlie Harding
The Fitzroy Nursery
In.cube8r

Quality Australian Designed & Manufactured Playground Equipment

Unit 16 / 459 Tufnell Rd, Banyo QLD 4014 Call : 1300 132 047 www.willplay.com.au

URBIS
DESIGNING SUSTAINABLE FUTURES
Urbis connects the brightest people to shape cities and communities for a better future.
Learn more at urbis.com.au

OCULUS
MELBOURNE
SYDNEY
WASHINGTON
www.oculus.info
australia@oculus.info

Kerb #1

Kerb #2

Kerb #3

Kerb #4

Kerb #5

Kerb #6

Kerb #7

Kerb #8

Kerb #9

Kerb #10

Kerb #11

Kerb #12

Kerb #13
Gaps

Kerb #14

Kerb #15
Landscape Urbanism

Kerb #16
Future Cities

Kerb #17
Is LA Dead?

Kerb #18
Plasticity, Fantasticity

Kerb #19
Paradigms of Nature:
Postnatural Futures

Kerb #20
Speculative Stories

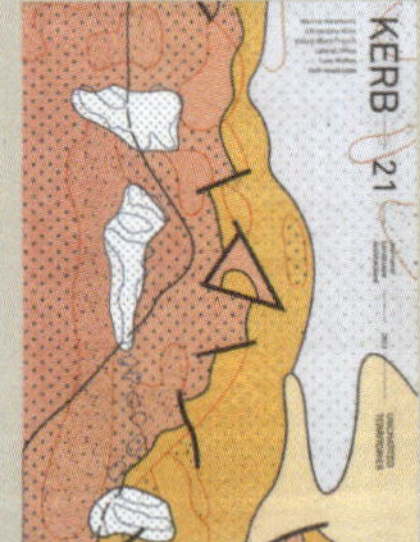

Kerb #21
Unchartered Territories

Kerb #22
Remoteness

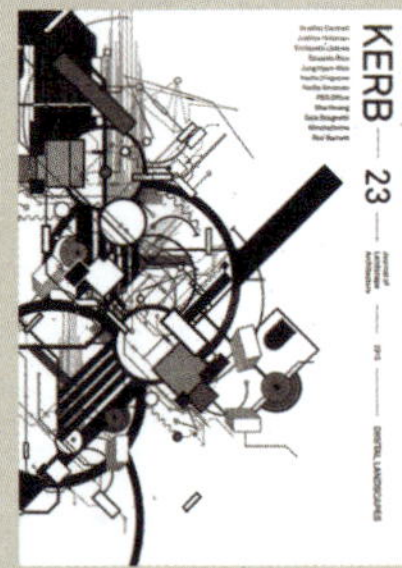

Kerb #23
Digital Landscapes

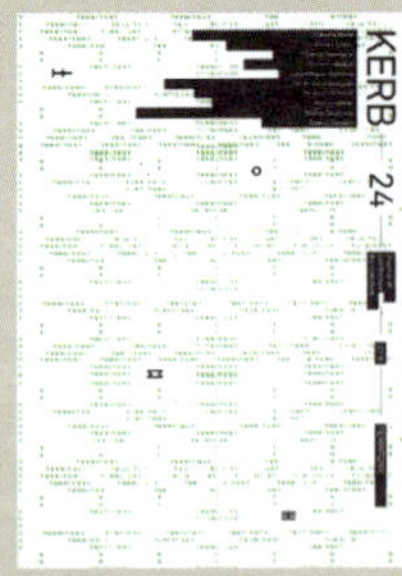

Kerb #24
Territory

Kerb #25
Contested Landscapes /
Disruptive Practice